A BETTER

ME

IN HIM

...born to prosper

Vincent K. Kpodo

Unless otherwise noted, all scriptures are from the King James Version of the Holy Bible.

For Vincent K. Kpodo

vincentkpodo.com

vincentkpodo.org

ISBN-13: 978-0-9992105-1-2

DEDICATION

This book is dedicated to Amanda my virtuous wife, whose picture is on the cover of this book, my Father: Linus F. K. Kpodo, my beautiful Mother: Bridget Castel Kpodo, Tehillah my daughter, Lina and the rest of my siblings, the Castel family, my Jethro from Texas, all my mentors, partners, helpers and leaders of the Generation of Faith Foundation and Prayer Network. It is my prayer that this book will equip you to become a better "you" in Him.

TABLE OF CONTENTS

ACKNOWLEDGMENTS

Without His Inspiration, I would not have been able to share this with you; I therefore express my sincerest gratitude to Our Precious Holy Spirit. The aphorism, "Behind every successful man, there is a woman," is made evident in my works. Without Amanda, I would not have had the peace of mind to make this a success; thank you for being a virtuous woman and a great mother to Tehillah our daughter.

To Jamillah, Patricia, Unyime and everyone who actively contributed to the success of this project, I am grateful. To all the men and women who have constantly made themselves available to mentor, coach and support me in one way or the other, THANK YOU.

To the wonderful staff, leaders, partners and friends of the Generation of Faith Foundation and the Generation of Faith Prayer Network: YOU ALL ARE THE FINEST. Keep pressing on as we make our God and His works more known in a practical way.

INTRODUCTION

14 BECAUSE HE HATH SET HIS LOVE UPON ME, THEREFORE WILL I DELIVER HIM: I WILL SET HIM ON HIGH, BECAUSE HE HATH KNOWN MY NAME. 15 HE SHALL CALL UPON ME, AND I WILL ANSWER HIM: I WILL BE WITH HIM IN TROUBLE; I WILL DELIVER HIM, AND HONOUR HIM. 16 WITH LONG LIFE WILL I SATISFY HIM, AND SHEW HIM MY SALVATION.

PSALM 91:14-16

I am grateful that God has led you to these words at this time! I was teaching on the Prayer Network not too long ago about some of the factors that bring accelerated results in prayer. In that discussion, I also pointed out some issues that can hinder your prayers from being answered quickly.

The teachings I conducted, for which this book was inspirationally written, are called "Born to Prosper" and "For Zion's Sake I Will Excel."

"For Zion's sake will I not hold my peace, and for Jerusalem's sake I will not rest, until the righteousness thereof go forth as brightness, and the salvation thereof as a lamp that burneth."

Isaiah 62:1

In the Holy Bible, Zion represents the Kingdom of God and His chosen people that He loves. When God delivered Zion, He did so **suddenly**. As believers, we are adopted and reborn into the Body of Christ. Irrespective of the hardships or challenges that you may

face, God is able to deliver you **SUDDENLY.** We must not let anything get in the way of our relationship and connection with God. As a matter of fact, the most important person needed in our network is God. At every level in life, everyone needs God!

> The most important person needed in our network is God.

Maintaining a prayer centered life is essential in keeping us well rooted in God and His purpose for our lives. It must be done in Spirit and in Truth, with the right motives, and must be in accordance with His will for our lives.

Prayer is a sacred act that gives us constant access to God. It is one of the strongest tenets of Christianity and should be practiced with passion in order to bring forth life changing results.

I strongly believe that prayer is a commandment from God. It is clearly shown in scripture how Jesus instructed us to pray at all times.

"And he spake a parable unto them to this end, that men ought always to pray, and not to faint";
Luke 18:1

Prayer is actually one way of expressing our love towards God. If you love someone, you would want to spend quality time with them. As a matter of fact, the greatest commandment of all is to "love the Lord your God with all your heart, and with all your soul, and with all your mind (Read Matthew 22:37-38)."

So you see my friend, if you truly love God, you will yearn to spend quality time with Him in prayer. A relationship is not a one way street and should not be based on self-interest alone. I do not know of too many people who have remained in a relationship that is based on selfish interest.

In that same manner, it is important that when we go to God in prayer, we do not only focus on ourselves (our selfish desires) alone but rather focus on God's agenda. It is also a first commandment to love God with all your heart, soul and mind and secondly to love your

neighbor as yourself.

When you pray, you must truly go after the heart of God. Only sincere love and reverence for God can bring you close to Him. Touching the heart of God will bring healing, transformation and solutions to many problems; without it, you cannot prosper.

Ecclesiastes 12: 13-14 indicates that the whole duty of man is to fear God and obey His commandments. This scripture further emphasizing that God judges everything overt and/or secret. This means actions, deeds and intentions (good or bad) are made known to God.

If you love God, you will obey His commandments and be concerned about living a life that is satisfying to Him. Operating in fear of God shows that you love and honor Him. This demonstration of love draws an intimate relationship and allows you to further your walk in His wisdom.

All your actions must express fear and reverence for God, including your prayers. God

is fully aware of the reason why you are praying the types of prayers you are praying and desiring the things you desire. Are you praying for the edification of God's Kingdom and will, or yourself? There is no secret or motive (pure or impure), that can be hidden from our God.

When seeking God, your heart must be right. A pure and contrite heart God will not despise (Psalm 51:17). When you harbor impure motives, revenge, retaliation, hatred or un-forgiveness in your heart, your Spirit becomes contaminated. An unclean heart can hinder your prosperity and blessings, pushing good success away from you.

Operating in disobedience, ignorance, un-forgiveness or laziness, etc., will block you from achieving success. These aforementioned things can create mental, spiritual, emotional, physical health and financial issues, and further place limits on your ability to prosper. Also, they prevent your prayers from being answered quickly by God.

God desires that His children prosper in life

and be in good health (3 John 1:2). He desires for you to be healed, delivered and able to prosper and excel in all areas of life. The enemy knows this and will try by any means possible to stop you; using internal and external forces (including your own self) to hinder your blessings.

If you have a spiritually contaminated heart, it will be seen and judged by God. This will be a major factor that prevents the power of God from flowing into your life. When we come before God in prayer and worship, it must only be done in spirit and in truth. A polluted Spirit has the ability to place a barrier on you reaching the heart of God; it takes the right conditions.

Therefore, you must invite God in and grant Him permission to clean the dirty things in your life. Be truly determined to take the necessary steps to release everything that contaminates your heart, and aim to have a good standing with God. Otherwise you will be prone to oppression and manipulation by the

enemy.

To have a good relationship with God: (1) you must love Him with your whole heart, mind and soul; love Him because of who He is... "your heavenly Father." (2) Trust, believe and do not doubt Him. (3) He must be kept first in your decision making and all that you do in life. Giving thanks and appreciation starts daily before your feet touch the floor. (4) Worship and prayer is not simply a daily routine but a continuous way of life. (5) His will is a <u>priority</u>; (6) and you are <u>obedient</u> to His commandments.

As the word of God teaches us, when you acknowledge God in all you do, He will direct your path. Have you ever wondered why it seems that some people can pray and receive quick results while others do not? There are different things that can interfere with the desired answer to your prayers.

This book will point out these areas that have the ability to block your prayers, and discuss how to overcome them. Additionally,

sample prayer points are included that you can add to your prayers.

It is important to let nothing interfere with the effectiveness of your prayers. Prayer can positively change the course of your destiny and should not be taken for granted.

VINCENT KPODO

CHAPTER ONE

BORN TO PROSPER!

"BELOVED, I WISH ABOVE ALL
THINGS THAT THOU MAYEST
PROSPER AND BE IN GOOD HEALTH,
EVEN AS THY SOUL PROSPERETH."

3 JOHN 1:2

You were born to prosper! Prosperity is inclusively connected to your abundance in life. Do you know that God has your best interest at heart and wants you to prosper? Furthermore, He commands it; yes, prosperity is a command from God! Jeremiah 29:11 states, "For I know the plans I have for you, declares the LORD, plans to prosper you and not to harm you, plans to give you hope and a future."

When God created man, it was done in His image and likeness. The first commandment He declared was for man to have dominion over the earth and to be fruitful, multiply, and subdue the earth (Genesis 1: 26-28). This instruction was not a suggestion nor recommendation; it was a command given by God.

Everything God made was designed to reproduce more of itself, bring increase, multiply and be fruitful- having the capability to flourish on earth. One of the requirements for man to operate in the likeness of God is having the attributes of prosperity and actually prospering. The ability to be fruitful, multiply

and subdue the earth cannot be done without it.

You Are Commanded To Prosper

Henceforth, using the Law of First Mentions, we can reasonably deduce that prosperity for the believer is a foundational commandment from God. The kind of prosperity God desires for us could figuratively be described as a level of prosperity to the nth degree; it is beyond the imagination of mankind.

Prosperity in operation brings increase, multiplication, and fruitfulness. Therefore, in giving this commandment, God shows that His divine and original plan is for man to be prosperous and flourish in life.

With the restoration of the authority to dominate the world through Christ Jesus in mind, WE CAN DO ALL THINGS to include the ability to prosper and fulfill this commandment. God wants us to live blessed and prosperous lives. Even when we get off track He is able to bring us back on track,

connecting us with the right people and resources necessary to ensure the fulfilment of this agenda. WHAT A MIGHTY GOD WE SERVE!!!

The "God Kind of prosperity" requires a partnership (relationship). Without a doubt, the best partnership (relationship) you can have is with God. In every partnership (relationship) there are expectations, agreements and boundaries, where faithfulness and trustworthiness are significant qualities.

When we have a partnership with God we agree to love what He loves and hate what He hates; two can only walk together if they agree (Amos 3:3; Romans 12:9; Psalm 97:10; Deuteronomy 10:12). When you value the relationship, you want to do everything possible to preserve it.

Therefore, the authenticity of your relationship with God will allow "the God Kind of prosperity" to activate and continuously keep flourishing. As great of a partner He is, He does

everything possible to prevent that partnership from being destroyed by any foreign agent (the enemy). For as long as we let Him, He will help us with the grace to resist the enemy who in turn desires to lure us into breaching our partnership with God.

Since we are born again in Jesus Christ, we owe ourselves the responsibility to live a prosperous life. We are under command to be fruitful in all that we do in our daily lives.

During my over 10 years of service in the United States Military, I have placed many people under command and have also been placed under command on countless occasions. One fact about being placed under command is that you are left with no other choice but to do what you are commanded to do.

Although some of the tasks may seem almost impossible, the fact that you have been placed under command means you need to do everything possible to complete that task. In a like manner, as the military, I believe this is

what God did to us when He commanded us to be fruitful; it is a task we must fulfill.

You Were Born To Prosper

Let's go deeper. John 1:1 clearly states that in the beginning was the word and Jesus Christ is the word made flesh. So, if Jesus is the word and we have become one with Him, whomsoever joins with Him also becomes a word from God and has His attributes (likeness). God states that His Word shall not return unto Him void, but that it shall accomplish that which He pleases.

Therefore, since we are a word from God, we are mandated to be prosperous. In order to see this brought into physical manifestation, we must pray the commandment of God upon our lives; that we will prosper and the anointing of growth and fruitfulness will rest upon our lives in every area. Furthermore, anything blocking our ability to prosper- be uprooted and cut off from our lives, in Jesus' name.

Having a well-grounded prayer life is

imperative for living a life of prosperity. However, know that character traits cannot be ignored. There are some personal attributes that can hinder your blessings and push "good success" away from you, which ultimately limits you from walking in prosperity.

For example, one attribute is operating with wrong motives. We study in scripture that man looks at the outward appearance but the Lord looks at the heart (read 1 Samuel 16:7). James 4:3 also declares "When you ask, you do not receive, because you ask with wrong motives, that you may spend what you get on your pleasures."

With these two scriptures in perspective, we can reasonably conclude that having the wrong motive is a big hindrance to obtaining and living a prosperous life. Having the right character (which includes the right motives) dappled with a good and sincere prayer life puts you in the right position to receive the creative ideas and all that is needed to prosper in life. For God's eyes are upon the righteous and His

ears are open to their prayers: but the face of the Lord is against them that do evil (Peter 3:12).

Evil deeds, desires and conceptions will definitely prevent one from receiving desired results from God which in turn repels you from the God-kind of prosperity. Your heart, intentions, choices, actions, character and other attributes must reflect the manifestation of the will of God, which include following His commandments. In doing so, you place yourself in the right position to have your prayers answered by God and hence clear the path that leads to a prosperous life.

Joshua 1:8 says "This book of the law shall not depart out of thy mouth; but thou shalt meditate therein day and night, that thou mayest observe to do according to all that is written therein: for then thou shalt make thy way prosperous, and then thou shalt have good success."

You see, not only does God want us to prosper but rather, He wants us to have Good

Success; He wants us to succeed beyond our imagination. Trying to reconcile the God-Kind of Good Success with our mortal minds is almost impossible but God is a God of possibilities. HE IS ABLE!!! All we need to do is to trust Him at His Word and work towards it.

Poverty Is Evil

As God desires for us to prosper, the enemy wants the opposite, POVERTY! Poverty is an enemy and a negative force behind Satanic operations. It represents lack, "in need of" and "not enough of," to where extra help is needed. It is the goal of poverty to disgrace and embarrass the believer.

Growing up in Ghana, West Africa, I witnessed many brilliant, handsome young men (sometimes under the age of 10 years old) who skipped school to join their mothers in selling food in the local markets with aspirations of making enough money to feed the family for that day and pay their school tuition.

Unfortunately, some of them never returned to school... This is indeed an evil act of poverty to disgrace an entire family. As a child, I literally witnessed many potentially great lives go into shambles because of poverty. THIS ENEMY IS REAL!!!

I declare that any spirit of poverty sent to disrupt your life be bound and cast out in Jesus' Name!!! Poverty is the primary method by which Satan steals, kills and destroys your prosperity.

> Poverty is the primary method by which Satan steals, kills and destroys your prosperity.

By inflicting one with poverty, the enemy opens the door for continuous mental, spiritual, emotional, physical, financial, occupational, educational and other strongholds to limit your abundance in life and ability to prosper.

It does not stop there. These strongholds bring along many forms of addiction, anxiety, depression, anger, bitterness, retrogression in life, repetitive cycles, and failure, only to

mention a few.

Poverty is a tactic often camouflaged to attack many areas in the lives of people. Poverty can be very deceiving in looks and operation. It could easily creep into your life only to be detected at the 11th hour if so. As a believer, there is therefore a high need to be vigilant as a serpent (read Matthew 10:16).

In Proverbs 24:33-34, we are told that "a little sleep, a little slumber, a little folding of hands to sleep: So shall thy poverty come," so you see, the spirit of poverty is constantly seeking where it may reside. Don't let him in!!!

Poverty Can Cause You To Suffer

Whenever the word poverty is mentioned, the initial thought is finances or economic status. However, poverty can also represent LACK, SHORTAGE, DEFICIENCY AND DEPRIVATION of necessary resources. Poverty can affect our ability to function well physically, financially, spiritually, mentally and emotionally—this is known as 'collective lack.'

The examples below show a variety of ways by which poverty can appear in our lives:

- **Impoverished Thinking**: This is a kind of mental poverty where the enemy's main target is one's mind. Someone with impoverished thinking lacks the ability to think with clarity, confidence and stability. Someone in this category deals with mental blockages which prevents them from having a sound mind. With this kind of defect, they are not able to experience the God-Kind of Peace that guards our mind. Because their mind, and therefore their life, is not stable—doubt, fear, and worry can take precedence over faith.

- **Inability to Love:** This is a serious case of poverty because the heart is the main target. Once the heart is infected, your words become infected as well which leads to undesired manifestations in your life (Luke 6:45; Proverbs 10:11; Matthew 12:34). Poverty in this area causes one to

have a heart that is severely restricted in its capacity to love. God is love and He has given us the most important commandment, which is to love God and love others (Read Matthew 22:37-39). Deficiency in the ability to love has a negative impact on all levels of life (Proverbs 4:23). Poverty in love results in physical and spiritual sickness. It is challenging for this person to identify authentic love, as well as receive or give it.

- **Un-forgiveness:** I call this the inability to forgive and let offenses go. If someone is unable to forgive the offenses of others, they will experience a blockage or delay in their prayers being answered. Their sins remain unforgiven (see Matthew 6:15) and they often embrace bitterness, hurt, anger, blame and excuses as a way of life. People in this category spend their precious time imagining the demise or downfall of those who offended them, meanwhile, that amount of time could have been spent

meditating on God's Word (read Joshua 1:8) or imagining/planning a prosperous activity. Those who fall under this category often lack the ability to live a happy life.

- **Disobedience:** Those who fall under this category often lack the wisdom (read Proverbs 9:10) to obey rules and meet expectations. There is no interest in following the commandments of God, the laws of the land or the directions of good advice and prophecy. The fear of God is often not present in such people. Operating in disobedience blocks the blessings of God from flowing in your life. In this case, the spirit of poverty is deployed to take over one's blessings by sometimes opening doors of embarrassment, shame and disgrace, increasing roadblocks and hardships. People of this nature usually learn the hard way and always through experience, if they learn at all.

- **Lack of Knowledge:** This is almost self-explanatory; people in this segment operate in ignorance, they are like the chaff that goes into the direction of the wind. Isaiah 5:13 says "therefore my people are gone into captivity, because [they have] no **knowledge**: and their honourable men [are] famished, and their multitude dried up with thirst." It is sad what ignorance can do to an entire nation; it brings disgrace, missed opportunities, famine, and blocked blessings. Poverty in this aspect is used to create hurdles which prevents forward movement in life. Many who lack knowledge live life in circles with little to no aspirations. They believe in luck rather than the Word and Promises of God.

- **Lack of Ambition:** People who are lazy are often without ambition; ambition itself is a drive that keeps you motivated and ready to start each day with enthusiasm and confidence. Someone in this category lacks the motivation to thrive and become

successful. It interferes with mental stamina and discipline to utilize time wisely. Poverty has succeeded in encouraging slothfulness instead of action by causing people to focus on how they feel (unworthy, incapable, fearful, weak), and causing them to reach for excuses as to why they can't accomplish their goals. People in this segment have not recognized the value of time and the law of sowing and reaping.

- **Poor Health:** When one's health is weakened by physical, mental and emotional afflictions. 'Dis-ease' causes disease. Someone with this condition has allowed poverty to rob their health, physical endurance and spiritual strength. Those who are facing this issue are unable to experience peace, joy and happiness in its fullness.

The aforementioned examples were given to show how poverty can covertly strike in one's life. When children of God do not walk in the

fullness of who they are supposed to be, with the attributes and characteristics of Christ, they are experiencing spiritual deprivation (poverty) in some area. This means that there is an area in their spiritual life where the power and glory of God is not overflowing. It is therefore my prayer that God will cause His power to overflow in every area of your life in Jesus' Name!

It is imperative to consistently pray against the mission statement of the enemy (steal, kill, and destroy according to John 10:10); simply put, the enemy wants to give believers the direct opposite of what God wants. He is the father of lies, there is no truth in him (John 8:44). He presents his schemes and devices in a camouflaged and counterfeit form in order to deceive.

Poverty Is Not From God

Poverty aims to hinder your success in many forms and your ability to prosper, even in your prayer life. The enemy knows that God wants

to prosper, heal and deliver you; therefore, he tries to block you by any means necessary, keeping you distracted and encouraging you to move into the dark places in life.

The good news is that if your life falls into any or all categories of poverty mentioned above, there is hope for you. Isaiah 43:19 declares "Behold, I will do a new thing; now it shall spring forth; shall ye not know it? I will even make a way in the wilderness, *and* rivers in the desert." God is able to turn every area of poverty in your life to an area of prosperity. As a matter of fact, no one can do it like He does it.

I am a firm believer in experiencing change through prayer and taking proactive actions. I encourage you to devote some time to praying specifically concerning these areas of your life and decide to change. James 4:7 says "Submit yourselves therefore to God. Resist the devil, and he will flee from you." Once you submit yourself and situation consciously to God, resisting the enemy by prayer and deeds, you

are rest assured of your answer.

It is vital to examine and identify the characteristics and attributes of Poverty that might be hindering you; God does not want us ignorant of the enemy's devices. Once that is done, take time to make sure that each area is addressed effectually and fervently in prayer (read James 5:16). Prayer should be done with great expectation and belief that the prayers will be answered (I John 5:14,15).

It wasn't until my wife became expectant in pregnancy that we had the privilege of parking right in front of the doors(literally) at the entrance of the hospital; this saved us a long walk from the main parking decks. Not everyone could park there; these were reserved parking spaces for "expectant mother only." These parking spaces were always there and of course very convenient, but we could only get access to it because we were "expecting"; we met the qualifications to receive this privilege. In other words because you are a child of God you should have expectations, know your

qualifications and privileges.

Your level of expectancy in life goes a long way to determine what you receive. As a born again child of God and joint heir with Jesus Christ, what is your expectancy? No level of poverty should be tolerated in the life of a born again believer. Begin to walk around boldly in great expectation because the Lord is our Shepard WE SHALL NOT WANT!

Prayers from Chapter One

Scripture: Proverbs 3:5-6 [5] Trust in the Lord with all thine heart; and lean not unto thine own understanding.[6] In all thy ways acknowledge him, and he shall direct thy paths.

Prayer Points:

1. Like Ruth, lead me to the right harvest field.

2. I declare that we are stepping into our place of wealth

3. I do not want to go where you do not want me to go.

4. I want to be in your perfect will.

5. I do not want to do things my own way.

6. I do not want to struggle in areas I do not have to struggle.

7. I am a commandment from the Lord.

8. I am a word from the Lord.

9. I will not die but fulfill that which the Lord said.

10. I will accomplish that which the Lord said I will accomplish.

11. I will prosper and be fruitful in my going out and my coming in. Where the sole of my feet go, I will prosper according to the Word of God.

12. Spirit of fruitfulness overtake me in the name of Jesus.

13. I decree and declare I am becoming fruitful.

14. I declare that I am fruitful in every area of my life.

15. I declare that any agent of poverty sent to disgrace me be arrested in Jesus' Name.

16. I declare that the curse of poverty is broken of my life by the Blood of Jesus.

17. I announce my freedom from the bondage of poverty in Jesus' Name.

18. I declare that the ideas needed to prosper are coming to me in Jesus' Name.

19. I declare that any spirit of poverty sent to disrupt my life be bound and cast out in Jesus' Name!!!

20. I declare that I am blessed and highly favored in Jesus' Name!

CHAPTER TWO

MOTIVES

¹³ LET US HEAR THE CONCLUSION OF
THE WHOLE MATTER: FEAR GOD,
AND KEEP HIS COMMANDMENTS:
FOR THIS IS THE WHOLE DUTY OF
MAN. ¹⁴ FOR GOD SHALL BRING
EVERY WORK INTO JUDGMENT, WITH
EVERY SECRET THING, WHETHER IT
BE GOOD, OR WHETHER IT BE EVIL .
ECCLESIASTES 12:13-14

A few years ago, there was a group of people who assisted me periodically with my ministerial projects; these were tenacious believers. They often spoke very well of me and offered to do things that I did not ask them to do at their own expense; UNDENIABLY GREAT PEOPLE! I loved and treated them very well to the best of my abilities.

However, for some odd reason, I kept discerning something fishy about them; I just could not seem to put my hand on it. One day in a night vision, I saw a few evil looking creatures with scary, weird, and creepy faces around me in a circular form while I was in the middle. As I curiously began to look at these creatures, their faces started taking the form of human beings.

The faces that I saw in the vision were similar to the faces of some of these "helpers." I woke up in the morning very thankful for this vision because it came in a time when I needed to make some really important decisions and life changing adjustments to the organizational

structure. In fact, I was considering a few of them as potential candidates. Without this revelation, I would have probably appointed one of them for a strategic position which could have caused a huge setback to our operations. Even though these people seemed to be for me, their hearts were not for me; their motives were off.

Motives Are Linked To One's Heart

In my opinion, **one of** the greatest gifts is the ability to see the motives of people. Because the motives of those "false helpers" were revealed to me, I made a lot of "room to err" for them and eventually, they slowly but surely unveiled their true characters. They dropped the ball in many areas but I had already made more than enough room for them to err because the Lord had already revealed it.

Because of this, I was not agonized by their actions at all. Knowing the motives of people often helps in guarding your heart. This kind of gift only comes from God through our Precious

Holy Spirit. Not everyone who speaks enticing words to you is for you. This is one reason why you are prone to getting hurt when you choose to deal with people **solely in the natural**.

One thing that many people do not pay attention to is the "unspoken words" of people. God, through His prophet, said in Isaiah 29:13 that "these people come near to me with their mouth and honor me with their lips, but their hearts are far from me. Their worship of me is based on merely human rules they have been taught."

Apostle Paul said that God "will bring to light what is hidden in darkness and will expose the motives of the heart" (Read 1 Corinthians 4:5, NIV); it is therefore obvious that God has access to the motives of everyone.

Now, if God has full access to the hearts of men, which is a **tank** for the "unspoken words" or motives of people, I believe that it will behoove us to stay very close to Him if we want Him to show us the hidden agenda (motives) of people. One major way of staying close to God

is through prayer. By doing so, you will gain an upper hand in all your transactions with people, and it will prevent you from easily getting hurt. Jesus Christ was not offended when Judas betrayed Him because He had fore-knowledge about it.

The truth of the matter is that we are all spirit beings trying to live right in a natural body. Therefore, there is always a struggle which makes us prone to making mistakes.

Ignoring the spiritual aspect of your dealings with others makes you subject to being controlled by either your selfish agenda or the agenda of other people with all kinds of wicked and hidden motives. It is said better in Jeremiah 17:9 that "the heart is deceitful above all things, and desperately wicked; who can know it?"

> The heart is the kitchen where motives are cooked.

Motives are deeply connected to matters of one's heart. As a matter of fact, the heart is the kitchen where motives are cooked. Motives can be defined as the driving force influencing your

behavior, whether good or bad. It is an incentive that pushes you to accomplish your goals. Motives are seeds that birth many actions in life.

Good Motives and Bad Motives

> Motives are seeds that births many actions in life.

Motives can center around things that are good and pleasing to God such as being helpful to others and working on personal, spiritual, educational, and occupational goals. On the other hand, motives can be linked to negativity and things that do not edify. Evil schemes, manipulations, greed, pride, envy,

plots to retaliate, and selfishness are all attributes of wrong motives.

Bad motives camouflage an array of deceptions, and requires operating in the

dark; it does not reflect the love of God. Walking in the light and love of God requires clean and pure motives.

Walking with the right motive leads to

prosperity, peace, and "good success," whereas having the wrong motives leads to mental poverty and many more. Someone impacted by mental poverty entertains the wrong voice which leads them down the wrong path. The voices you heed to determines which direction you go in life.

As Children of God, distinguishing between the voice of God and the voice of the enemy is very vital. John 10:27 states, "my sheep hear my voice, and I know them, and they follow me." Neglecting or not knowing the voice of God is like a child who cannot hear his mother's voice.

Voices lead and direct us in life; therefore if the voice of the Father is not leading you, it is obvious where you will be headed in life. You might be on a path that looks good in your eyes but is actually the wrong path because you are being led by the wrong voice.

The wisest King of old during his ruler-ship said "there is a way that seems right to unto a man, but the end thereof are the ways of death

(Proverbs 14:12)."

Dr. Myles Munroe said "the number one enemy of right is good." The wrong voice will get you to do some good stuff which might not be the right stuff for you. Be careful of the voices that you allow in your ears.

Before Christ called me, I used to drink and smoke excessively. All the friends (voices) that I had around me encouraged and cheered me on. We often said, "this is really good," "I would not trade this good stuff for nothing," and many more.

Unbeknown to me, those voices were leading me to death!!! It seemed good at that time but it was not the right thing for me. All these things took place because I was listening to the wrong voices. It is a necessity that the voice of God echoes louder than any other voice in our life.

In 1 Samuel 17, Goliath, an uncircumcised Philistine, tormented the children of God for forty consistent days. Day after day Goliath would go against the children of God and

everyone was scared and unable to take a stand against him. Goliath was speaking into the ears of God's people and scaring them with his voice. He brought fear upon the land through his "voice."

The Voice of God Must Echo Louder Than Any Other Voice

Many people today are frightened by the many evil tormenting voices in the land; some of these voices introduce the fear of sickness, disease, suicide, poverty, shame, pain, regrets, revenge, jealousy, pride, hatred etc.

These voices could be likened to the voice of Goliath tormenting. Hebrews 12:24 says that the blood of Jesus "speaketh better things than the blood of Abel"; it is therefore clear that the Precious Blood of Jesus has a voice.

In a room filled with many voices, the loudest and most influential voice prevails. In that same way, the "Voice of the Blood of Jesus" is powerful to the extent that it is able to mute or shut down every voice that is speaking against

you. One effective way of enforcing this is through prayer.

David's reply to Goliath in 1 Samuel 45-46 was, *"Thou comest to me with a sword, and with a spear, and with a shield: but I come to thee in the name of the Lord of Hosts, the God of the armies of Israel, whom thou hast defied."* This shows that you can also speak to the evil voices with the Word of God through prayer; YES, YOU CAN!!

David further said: [46] *"This day will the Lord deliver thee into mine hand; and I will smite thee, and take thine head from thee; and I will give the carcases of the host of the Philistines* <u>*this day*</u> *unto the fowls of the air, and to the wild beasts of the earth; that all the earth may know that there is a God in Israel. [47] And all this assembly shall know that the Lord saveth not with sword and spear: for the battle is the Lord's, and he will give you into our hands."*

David was tired of allowing the evil voice of Goliath to disgrace the people of God because

he knew how powerful our God is. He finally had enough and said "THIS DAY"; I believe there comes a time in your life when you have to declare to the enemy that enough is enough, "THIS DAY......!!" "THIS DAY.......!!" "THIS DAY......!!"

David's example demonstrates that you have the power to make declarations and decrees concerning your position and prophesy to your own situation irrespective of how bad things might look. You see, David literally defeated Goliath with the Word of God. Do not underestimate the power of the Word of God. David knew how to battle strategically and it worked for him. He knew that if he placed God in the middle of the physical battle he would win.

Any time you put God first in your life, you are automatically set up to succeed. I always tell people in training that if you want to see quick results in prayer, let the motive behind your prayers be a major benefiting factor to the kingdom of God or the agenda of God.

This is why examining the God factor in your decisions and motives is so important. The God factor always comes with good motives and helps expedite your desired answers. On the other hand, operating with impure motives can block your prayers from being answered. Right motives in life will cause you to prosper and increase, but the wrong ones will eventually steal, kill, and destroy you.

What Motives Are Behind Your Actions?

The best way to minimize operating with the wrong motives is to examine yourself. Is your heart right? Do you treat others in the same manner that you desire to be treated? Why do you do the things you do? These are some of the questions you have to ask yourself on a daily basis.

Years ago, when Our Precious Holy Spirit started teaching me on motives, I found myself silently asking questions like, "what is my motive behind what I am about to say?" "How helpful is this thing or how helpful will it be?"

These silent questions really helped me to make the right decisions and say the right things.

Have you ever asked yourself what your motives towards God are? Do you seek God because you really Love and appreciate Him? Do you seek Him because you want a deeper meaning and relationship with Him? Or do you seek Him for what He will do for you? THESE ARE RELEVANT QUESTIONS THAT NEED TO BE ASKED.

There was a man in Luke 19:3 whose name was Zacchaeus. It is written of him that when he heard that Jesus was passing by, he "sought to see Jesus for **who He was.**" Unlike many who wanted to see Jesus because they desired healing or one breakthrough or another, Zacchaeus only wanted to see "**who He was.**"

This act caught the attention of Jesus to the extent that he decided to stay in his house. Seeking and worshipping God **for who He is** and not what He can give pushes Him to give us more than we desire.

Did you know that reaching the heart of God

with the right motives during prayer evokes the presence of God? Did you also know that in the presence of God there is a propensity of unveiling the unexpected? There is completeness, healing, added strength and transformation that only His presence can bring but it all begins with the right motive.

The right motives in life and during prayer sets you up for success on every good side. When you do things with the right intentions(motives), the Lord orders your steps. Living life with the right motives is an act of obedience to God's commandments, therefore it comes with a reward. When you place God at the center of your affairs and even your prayer life, you are bound to see a tremendous change in your life.

People that operate with the wrong motives in prayer to God usually experience mental poverty and challenges with receiving answered prayers. God is not man. He sees everything, therefore it is important that we stay honest and true (clean motives) to Him. God sees the

heart of man and this includes every unspoken word; that is why it is advised to render your heart and not your garments (Joel 2:13), for God is looking on the inside.

When operating with impure motives towards others, your supply of blessings are limited. Many people do not realize that the way they treat others, good or bad, is the way they are treating God (Matthew 25: 40-45).

Because we love God for who is He, our aim should be to always come before the Lord with the right heart and mind, good intentions and motives. In like manner, we must seek to relate to others with the right intentions and motives.

Prayers from Chapter Two

Scripture Reading: Psalm 51: 1-11

1Have mercy upon me, O God, according to thy lovingkindness: according unto the multitude of thy tender mercies blot out my transgressions. 2Wash me throughly from mine iniquity, and cleanse me from my sin. 3For I acknowledge my transgressions: and my sin is ever before me. 4Against thee, thee only, have I sinned, and done this evil in thy sight: that thou mightest be justified when thou speakest, and be clear when thou judgest. 5Behold, I was shapen in iniquity; and in sin did my mother conceive me. 6Behold, thou desirest truth in the inward parts: and in the hidden part thou shalt make me to know wisdom. 7Purge me with hyssop, and I shall be clean: wash me, and I shall be whiter than snow. 8Make me to hear joy and gladness; that the bones which thou hast broken may rejoice. 9Hide thy face from my sins, and blot out all mine iniquities.10Create in me a clean heart, O God; and renew a right spirit within me. 11Cast me not away from thy presence; and take not thy holy spirit from me.

Prayer Points:

1. Father in Heaven, I repent for operating with wrong motives.

2. Father, give me the wisdom to do things with the right motives from this day forward.

3. Father, please do not allow me to harbor any form of wrong motives in my heart against anyone

4. Create in me a clean heart, O God; and renew a right spirit within me.

5. I plead the blood of Jesus Christ to wash away everything that has contaminated—my mind, heart, body, spirit and soul.

6. Fill me with your spirit oh God and let lack and poverty be flushed out of every area of my life.

7. I bind the spirit of poverty and every stronghold that interferes with my

ability to prosper, in the name of Jesus.

8. Father in the name of Jesus, let the wrong motives of people around me be revealed to me.

9. Father, let the blood of Jesus cleanse me from impure motives and any form of mental poverty.

10. Today I renounce every evil voice aiming to influence my motives

11. Father, let the voice of the blood of Jesus be amplified over every other voice speaking evil into my life.

12. I declare that the power of the word of God has been activated in my life from this day forward.

13. I declare that my soul, body and spirit has been placed under the authority of the power of the Holy Ghost and therefore anything that is not pleasing to God cannot dwell in me.

14. I declare that my steps are ordered by the Lord and I will move according to His will in the mighty name of Jesus.

15. I declare that I will know the voice of God like I know the voice of my friends, in Jesus' Name.

16. In the name of Jesus let evil motives that are not pleasing to God be eliminated.

17. I declare that my motives are pleasing to God.

18. I declare that I will operate with the right motives from this day forward in the name of Jesus.

19. Father, I ask that you give me a mind like Christ that is pleasing to you.

20. I declare that I will seek the heart of God in the name of Jesus.

21. I declare from this day forward that I will have the right mind and heart that is pleasing to God in the name of Jesus.

22. In the name of Jesus let anything that is hindering my ability to operate with the right motives be destroyed by fire.

CHAPTER THREE

UN-FORGIVENESS

DO NOT SAY, "I WILL REPAY EVIL";
WAIT FOR THE LORD, AND HE WILL
DELIVER YOU.
PROVEBS 20:22

Unknown to many, forgiveness is a key to good success. Un-forgiveness on the other hand hinders the manifestation of the "God-Kind of Success (good success)." Un-forgiveness is a time waster imposed by the enemy to delay you in life.

Those who harbor un-forgiveness in their hearts tend to spend a lot of time trying to "repay evil" according to Proverbs 20:22. In other words, instead of being productive, they waste time plotting against those who did them wrong. This is not the will of God for the life of any believer. God wants you to become more productive and successful.

We read in scripture of how Jesus was more successful in His ministry than all of His disciples during His time. Even though the disciples had power, there was a level of success Jesus had that His disciples did not.

For instance, after the mountain of transfiguration, Jesus was approached by a man with a demon possessed boy. He explained to Jesus that he had brought his son to be

healed by His disciples while He was away on the mountain but the disciples were not successful at this (they could not heal him).

Jesus was able to successfully deliver the boy and heal him. Nevertheless, the disciples were confused as to why they were not successful in casting out the demon. They privately asked Jesus to explain why they failed. His response was because of little faith, unbelief, and their lack of effective fasting and prayer (Mathew 17:20, Luke 9:41, and Mark 9:29).

Prayer Was Very Much A Part Of Jesus' Daily Lifestyle

Out of the factors (faith, unbelief, fasting and prayer) listed above that led to Jesus' success, I would like to focus briefly on prayer. Prayer was very much a part of Jesus' daily lifestyle. As a matter of fact, after close observation of the daily routine of Jesus, His disciples noticed that He would normally return home from prayer while they were just waking up or sometimes long after they had woken up in the morning.

It was simply a part of His lifestyle (Luke 6:12; Mark 1:35). They knew that Jesus would always go to pray but they were not sure how to pray so they decided to ask Him to teach them also how to pray. It was at this point that Jesus started teaching His disciples extensively on **forgiveness** which is **a key to answered prayer and therefore a key to "good success."**

We see another success story in Mark 11:20-26 where Peter realizes that a fig tree had withered away because Jesus cursed it earlier. Peter at this point is startled by the successful works of Jesus, draws His attention to it, and Jesus begins to outline the recipe for this kind of success:

1. Have faith in God

2. Speak to it (whatever "it" may be) or pray about what you desire

3. Don't doubt; only believe in what you say or pray about

4.   NOW THE ULTIMATE ONE,

Forgive so that God will also **forgive** you

These four steps gave Jesus success in that case of the fig tree. The art

> The art of forgiveness is reciprocal

of forgiveness is reciprocal; it endorses you to become a candidate for speedy results.

Forgiveness unlocks the mercy of God in your life which ultimately

> Forgiveness unlocks the mercy of God in your life

leads to a prosperous life. Following the principles of God to include the principle of forgiveness definitely leads to a prosperous life.

It seems as though the principle or art of forgiveness is one that needs to be mastered in order to see consistent results in life. In one of my books on prayer, I write extensively on un-forgiveness and how it is a major, if not the number one, hindrance of the prayers and blessings of people. Jesus makes clear in Matthew 6:14-15 that if you forgive, your Father in Heaven will forgive you also but if you

do not forgive, neither will your Father in Heaven forgive you.

Giving With An Un-forgiving Heart

Therefore, if you bring your gift to the altar, and there remember that your brother has something against you, 24 leave your gift there before the altar, and go your way. First be reconciled to your brother, and then come and offer your gift.

Matthew 5:23-24

Offense and un-forgiveness can cause even your good deeds to become an abomination before God. When you harbor un-forgiveness in your heart your gifts are rejected by God. Wow; this means that God is more interested in a forgiving heart than your gift.

No wonder His word says in 1 Samuel 15:22 that obedience is better than sacrifice. Many times, we do things in an effort to please God but He wants our heart (where obedience begins). God speaks through His Prophet Joel by saying, "render your heart (the place where

forgiveness takes place) and not your garments (your gifts and outward appearances) (Joel 2:13)."

Now, a "gift given" is like a "seed planted" and whenever a seed is planted, harvest is expected. The kind of seed (gift) you plant determines the kind of harvest you receive. With this in mind, if the seed (gift) planted is acceptable in the sight of God, you can rest assured of a good (successful) harvest. In that same manner, if the seed (gift) planted is considered an abomination in the sight of God, you can imagine what you will reap.

God truly wants His Children to experience a great harvest; no wonder Jesus spent much time teaching on one of the major hindrances of these blessings which is "un-forgiveness."

I want you to look at un-forgiveness as sowing tares among your seedlings; the more you keep offense or harbor un-forgiveness, the more you stunt the growth of your seedlings and therefore delay your harvest if any. I want you to ask yourself this question. Is the offense

and un-forgiveness worth the blessing that is ahead of you? If no is your answer, then LET IT GO.

Un-forgiveness Attracts Negative Things

Un-forgiveness is a negative force that deprives you of your quality of life. I come across many people who think that the whole world is an evil place filled with evil people because they were once hurt and for some reason were not able to recover from it.

These people think everyone is out to get them. They see the negative in everything and attract the negative in everything. There are evil spirits that promote un-forgiveness and offense. Many people in the world today who commit suicide, mass shootings, and many murders do so as a result of offenses from their past and their inability to forgive.

I heard a story of a young lady who was advised by her mother to date any married man who desired to be with her. The reason behind her advice was because someone snatched her

husband from her years ago which led to a divorce and she never recovered. Unfortunately, her daughter ended up snatching another woman's husband as well; they got married only to find out years down the line that the man was an armed robber by profession.

A few years after their expensive wedding, the man was killed, leaving the new wife behind with young kids. Additionally, most of his properties were also seized by government authorities. What a tragedy! All this started with seeds of an offense and un-forgiveness.

The Stronghold of Offense and Un-forgiveness

Un-forgiveness is a major issue affecting the lives of many people. Many often find it challenging to forgive others or even themselves. The enemy capitalizes on this to wreak havoc in the lives of these people. Deciding to walk in forgiveness is a choice that has to be made daily.

After harboring many instances of un-forgiveness in the heart, it eventually becomes a stronghold. At this point, it controls many of your activities; it even affects how you see things.

No wonder Jesus commands us to constantly forgive no matter what. In response to a question of how many times you need to forgive someone, Jesus said to Peter in Matthew 18:21-22, "seventy-seven times." God wants us to forgive so that the enemy will not have this kind of stronghold in our life.

Unfortunately, what holds many people back from embracing forgiveness towards others is the evaluation of the offense—and the aftermath felt as the result of spiritual pain. It can be a difficult process to forgive but once you master the art of forgiveness, it becomes very simple. As a matter of fact, with the help of Our Precious Holy Spirit, you will not even get offended by the things that are meant to offend you.

Forgiveness is a necessary process for our own internal purification. If one holds on to un-forgiveness, their spirit becomes contaminated. A

> A contaminated spirit resists the blessings of God.

contaminated spirit cannot receive any good thing from God's uncontaminated spirit (Holy Ghost).

In other words, a contaminated spirit resists the blessings of God. People of this nature find themselves stagnated physically, emotionally, and spiritually. Most people look at forgiveness with their eyes fixed on what the other person did.

However, forgiveness should be more of a reflection from within (internal). Those who operate from a place of un-forgiveness routinely walk through their daily lives wounded, angry, and hurt. The ironic part of the lives of such people is that they end up wounding others, hurting others and being angry at others.

> You can only become conditioned to forgive by Our Holy Spirit and the Word of God.

On the other hand, those who are conditioned to forgive live a free life filled with laughter, happiness, and joy no matter what others do to them. The key is being conditioned to forgive. Every believer needs this type of conditioning. I tell you the truth: you can only become conditioned to forgive by Our Holy Spirit and the Word of God.

It is therefore very important to always pray that He helps you become conditioned to forgive even before offenses come. After you have been conditioned to forgive, internal judgment and a constant internal reminder will have to be used to help you walk in constant forgiveness.

Unfortunately, un-forgiveness keeps people in bondage. People stop growing and the lives, businesses, ministries, relations etc. of people comes to a standstill because of this bondage. One may think that forgiving is setting the

other person free, but in reality, the individual doing the forgiving is the one being set free from spiritual and emotional bondage.

It may appear that the transgressor may have escaped without being punished for what they have done, but if you lay the matter at God's feet to deal with, He will deal with it. He is a JUST and RIGHTEOUS God who has your best interest at heart. Let me put it this way, He said to Abraham in Genesis 12:3, "I will bless those who bless you and I will curse those who curse you."

Let Go and Let God

THAT IS YOUR WORD TODAY. Let go and let God handle it. Paul said in Galatians 6:7 "Be not deceived; God is not mocked: for whatsoever a man soweth, that shall he also reap." With all these scriptures available, why would you still want to hold things against people? I want you to trust God and His process.

> Forgiveness at any level is a process.

Know for a surety that He will fight for you when needed and His Spirit (our precious Holy Ghost) will also speak for you when needed; you just do your part and forgive. Also bear in mind that your refusal to forgive and let offenses go will hinder you in several ways.

Your petitions may be denied by God and you will not be forgiven of your own trespasses. Your joy, good health, good success and many more blessings stand a chance of being denied from you. **Is it worth it?**

Every believer must make it a mandate to

> What you do to others is directly done to God.

forgive and be kind as much as possible. It is not always easy to forgive but it is something that must be done. Jesus Christ on the cross ,after He had been brutalized and forsaken, still prayed in Luke 23:34 saying, "Father, forgive them, for they know not what they do." I want you to understand that what you do to others is directly done to God (Read Matthew 5:40; 1 John 4:4; Psalm 82:6); I know this sounds

simple but it is very true. It is not right to claim to love an unseen God (Yahweh) and mistreat the seen gods (God's representatives on earth).

Jesus said, "many will come saying Lord, Lord I did this in your name and Jesus will say depart from me I know you not (Matthew 7:21-23; Matthew 25:12)." I am sure you want to be in righteous standing before the Lord and therefore do not want this to be the case for you.

Once you catch the revelation that you are a representative of God and that everything you do to others affects God, you will have mastered half of the art of forgiveness. If we truly love God then we will love God's representatives on earth(mankind) and forgive them. May God grant you the grace and wisdom to let go and embrace the good even in those who hurt you.

Prayers from Chapter Three

Scripture : Ephesians 4: 31-32

[31] Let all bitterness, and wrath, and anger, and clamour, and evil speaking, be put away from you, with all malice: [32] And be ye kind one to another, tenderhearted, forgiving one another, even as God for Christ's sake hath forgiven you.

Scripture: 1John 1:9

[9] If we confess our sins, he is faithful and just to forgive us our sins, and to cleanse us from all unrighteousness.

Prayer Points:

1. Search me oh, Lord, if there be any un-forgiveness in my life or in my heart, take it out.

2. Father, I confess my inability to forgive, please forgive me for all the times I have not forgiven.

3. Father God, I choose to forgive, give me the grace to let go and release.

4. I confess (name) every hurt, shame, disappointment, rejection, offense and I release it from my mind, body, spirit and soul and let it go in the name of Jesus.

5. In the name of Jesus, I let go of all the pain from the past and I receive my complete healing, in the name of Jesus.

6. Un-forgiveness will not be a stronghold that remains in my life any longer.

7. I release un-forgiveness from my mind, heart and soul.

8. Father give me the grace to release un-forgiveness, let it not stop me from receiving my blessings.

9. Let the power of un-forgiveness be broken off of my life, in the name of Jesus, let it not hinder my breakthrough.

10. Father, help me to walk in the spirit of forgiveness.

11. In the name of Jesus I denounce hurt, bitterness, shame, anger, wrath, evil speaking, evil memories and associates with (list all events).

12. In the name of Jesus I release myself from un-forgiveness. I lay it all down at the feet of Jesus.

13. Let anything that is hindering my ability to forgive be destroyed by fire.

14. Father in Heaven, let my spirit be blocked from being contaminated.

15. Father help me to master the art of forgiveness.

16. Holy Ghost, please condition my mind and body to forgive.

17. Father give me the wisdom to constantly treat people right no matter how bad they treat me.

CHAPTER FOUR

LOVE

JESUS SAID UNTO HIM, THOU SHALT
LOVE THE LORD THY GOD WITH ALL
THY HEART, AND WITH ALL THY
SOUL, AND WITH ALL THY MIND.
THIS IS THE FIRST AND GREAT
COMMANDMENT. AND THE SECOND
IS LIKE UNTO IT, THOU SHALT LOVE
THY NEIGHBOUR AS THYSELF. ON
THESE TWO COMMANDMENTS HANG
ALL THE LAW AND THE PROPHETS.

MATTHEW 22:36

One of the recurring themes in the Bible is love. It is no surprise that when a Pharisee asked Jesus what the greatest commandment was, Jesus responded with "love." More precisely, Jesus stated that you must "Love the Lord your God with all your heart and with all your soul and with all your mind," and "Love your neighbor as yourself (Matthew 22:37-39)."

Love Is The Greatest Commandment

Not only is love considered the greatest of all commandments, it was also called a new commandment (John 13:34-35) **"A new commandment I give you: Love one another. As I have loved you, so also you must love one another)."** Love is a potent force and is at the essence of who God is. GOD IS LOVE (Read 1 John 4:8).

The love of God transcends beyond conditions, performance, or gain; the ultimate expression of this love was the sacrifice of God's only Son, Jesus Christ, on the cross for our salvation and redemption. His love transcends

so much to the extent that He forsook His Son just to express Himself (Love) to us as a sign of His love (Read John 3:16).

In 1 Corinthians 13: 4-7, Paul aptly describes love by saying: " Love is patient, love is kind. It does not envy, it does not boast, it is not proud. It does not dishonor others, it is not self-seeking, it is not easily angered, it keeps no record of wrongs. Love does not delight in evil but rejoices with the truth. It always protects, always trusts, always hopes, always perseveres." You see, as children of God, we are mandated to emulate the love of God to our fellow man.

Loving God and loving others increases our connection to God. It is undisputable that in a physical relationship where love is present, there is a high level of intimacy, affection, and the release of cherished information and gifts. The same thing applies to our relationship with God when we walk in **love**.

As we embrace love, we are actually embracing God. On the other hand, rejecting

love is rejecting God. God is the source of love and only through Him can love flow in us. Being unable to love is a sign that one is detached from God, because God is love.

As a son and daughter of God, you carry His name, "a child of God." The ability to operate in love demonstrates to others that you are a disciple of Christ. Jesus clearly states that anyone who claims to love God but fails to love their brother or sister is a liar (1 John 4:20).

God does not want you and I to be liars, He wants us to love. Essentially, He is saying that one should not claim to love a God whom they have never seen without loving their brother or sister who they see daily. Love is a lifestyle that reflects our true identity in God. Jesus, speaking of love as a lifestyle in John 13:35 said, "By this all men will know that you are My disciples, if you love one another."

You can tell the genuineness of someone by the love they often express. In many nations today people have started churches operating

with occult powers to exhibit strange miracles to draw people into their ministries.

In fact their acts are so deceiving that one could easily be lured to think that they are operating with the power of Jesus Christ. Some even use chemicals to ignite fire in services to make people think that they are powerful enough to call down fire from heaven like Elijah (this actually happened in a church in the southern part of Africa).

Others have also consulted occult powers and other powers of darkness to help them see spiritual things so that they can deceive many with all kinds of false prophecies. The list goes on and on and on but my point is that one element that will help you to distinguish the real from the fake is by observing the love that they express.

In Matthew 7:22-23, Jesus said: "On that day many will say to me, 'Lord, Lord, did we not prophesy in your name, and cast out demons in your name, and do many mighty works in your name?' 23 And then will I declare to them,

'I never knew you; depart from me, you workers of lawlessness." The truth is that because they have sold their souls to the enemy, they are not able to love like God commands.

Let No Situation Hinder Your Ability To Love

Jesus commands us in Matthew 5:44 to love our enemies and pray for those who persecute us. In this way, we can be perfect even as our Heavenly Father is perfect. The truth is that we cannot love as Jesus loved if we do not have the Spirit of God in us. I have personally realized that the only time that I am able to fully exhibit the love of God to others is when I have fully submitted my all to Him. When I first joined the military many years ago, I had a very thick accent but was also very hard working.

Everyone who saw me almost immediately knew that I was not only a minority but also an African with a thick accent yet I would not be quiet. I would often speak with a lot of people and always wanted to learn something new. I

even asked people to teach me how to speak like an American. Many of my colleagues often made a lot of smart and racist comments to and about me but I would always answer with a smile and pretend as if I did not hear their comment.

One day Leslie (a colleague) said to me "what's wrong with you? Why don't you respond rudely to them to set the record straight or report them to the Equal Opportunity Office?" I smiled at her and said don't worry. Within two years of being in that Battalion (a battalion typically consists of 300 to 800 soldiers), I was nominated the most outstanding soldier for the whole Brigade (a brigade is typically three to six battalions plus supporting elements as well).

Also, I was recommended to the promotion board during that time and I received the highest score, a score higher than even those who outranked me. What happened was that, the love of God through me overlooked all their

negative comments and kept pushing me to the top.

If God was to reveal your enemies to you, what would you do? Will you still love them? Would you treat them well? What about those that hurt, mistreat, lie and plot against you? Jesus Christ who knew Judas would betray Him still loved him and even placed him in charge of the finances of the ministry.

How you respond to your enemies goes a long way to determine if the love of God is operating in and through you or not. Because we are imperfect (Read Romans 3:23), we have to constantly strive to live a life filled with the radiating love of God. Without the Spirit of God in me at that time, I could not have loved them and overlooked their negative actions towards me. Without constantly striving to do so, it will become almost impossible to love like Jesus loved and loves.

Love is so essential that regardless of your spiritual gifts, ability to pray, prophesy, speak in tongues and give, if you lack love, it is all

done in vain (Read 1 Corinthians 13). You may be wondering, "What does love have to do with prosperity?" Love has everything to do with living a prosperous life. Proverbs 21:21 NIV declares that "Whoever pursues righteousness and love finds life, prosperity and honor."

Also, Deuteronomy 11:13-15 NIV states "So if you faithfully obey the commands I am giving you today-to love the LORD your God and to serve him with all your heart and with all your soul-then I will send rain on your land in its season, both autumn and spring rains, so that you may gather in your grain, new wine and olive oil. I will provide grass in the fields for your cattle, and you will eat and be satisfied."

These scriptures clearly denote that one fundamental key to prosperity is simply loving God and loving others with a sincere heart.

Between faith, hope and love, Love is the greatest so let us continually pray and ask God to teach us how to love Him and others just as He loves us.

Prayers from Chapter Four

Scripture: John 14:15 If ye love me, keep my commandments.

Prayer Points:

1. I repent from my refusal to love others as you have loved me.

2. Father increase me in the grace to walk in love.

3. In the name of Jesus, let any issue, situation, memory, or offense blocking my ability to love be uprooted out of my life in the name of Jesus Christ.

4. Father, please give me the wisdom to overlook the wrong doings of others against my life.

5. Father in Heaven, I ask that you cause your love to radiate through me wherever I go in Jesus' Name.

6. Father, make me an agent of love in Jesus' Name.

7. Father, make me an example of your love in Jesus' Name.

8. Help me to please you with my ways as a sign of my love for you.

9. Father I recognize the fact that you are Love, therefore as your child I ask that you teach me to love like you love.

10. In the Name of Jesus I shall prosper in love.

VINCENT KPODO

CHAPTER FIVE

IGNORANCE

⁶MY PEOPLE ARE DESTROYED FOR
LACK OF KNOWLEDGE: BECAUSE
THOU HAST REJECTED KNOWLEDGE, I
WILL ALSO REJECT THEE, THAT THOU
SHALT BE NO PRIEST TO ME: SEEING
THOU HAST FORGOTTEN THE LAW
OF THY GOD, I WILL ALSO FORGET
THY CHILDREN.

HOSEA 4:6

I am certain that if you were given the chance to go back to the age of ten with the knowledge and wisdom that you have today, you would make different choices in life. A great man once said, "you are the sum total of the choices you've made"; this is very true. We make choices each day, as a matter of fact it has been estimated according to internet sources that adults make 35,000 remotely conscious decisions daily (www.go.roberts.edu). Yes you read it correctly, 35,000!

> Ignorance is a limitation that makes the Lion think that it is in fact a Cat and therefore seeks someone to adopt him.

Each of these choices goes a long way to define us. The Bible declares in Hosea 4:6 that people are destroyed for lack of knowledge. Ignorance makes one unaware of the opportunities and blessings that God wants them to see and receive. Ignorance is a limitation that makes the Lion think that it is in fact a Cat and therefore seeks someone to adopt him. This

Lion spends its entire life in frustration because it is ignorant of its capabilities; on the other hand, no one adopts him because of his capabilities.

It is amazing what ignorance can do to a person. Ignorance can make you go into the grace with your untapped potentials in you but that is not the will of God for your life at all. Due to the fact that ignorance can keep you in the dark, your potential in life can also remain hidden from you just like the Lion who does not know it is a Lion.

Ignorance Brings Many Hardships

Ignorance can be one's greatest challenge in life. It is a mighty hinderer of blessings and good success. Because I travel around a lot, I get to meet and pray with many people. One prayer request that is almost consistent wherever I go is the prayer for direction. People want to know which step to take, where to go, what to do, who to get married to and many more. They are simply unaware of exactly what God wants them to do.

The enemy often uses the tactic of ignorance against the children of God. When one remains ignorant of the ways of God, they cannot enjoy the fulfillment of His benefits. The problem of ignorance did not just begin with this generation. In fact Jesus said in Luke 16:8 that *"the children of this world are in their generation wiser than the children of light."*

The good news is that God does not want us to remain ignorant. He wants us to be enlightened and full of insights. He wants us to be very well equipped for a prosperous life. The scriptures state in Romans 12:2 that we should not be conformed to this world but be transformed by the renewing of our mind, that we may prove what is good, and acceptable, and the perfect will of God. Therefore we must renew our minds with the Word of God in order to uproot every stronghold of ignorance from our lives.

There are numerous examples of how ignorance can be in operation in one's life. A common example with dangerous

consequences is when God blesses one with something new and wonderful and they refuse to let go of the old and wrong things. It is just like putting old wine in new wine skin or new wine in an old wine skin. Essentially, God tries to move one forward into greater blessings but they remain drawn to the obsolete.

When God Moves You Forward Ignorance Will Cause You To Look Back

For instance, there was a lady name Rhonda who only had single friends. She got married to the man of her dreams and performed her duties as a wife very well to the best of her abilities. In her spare time, especially when her husband was away, she would spend much time with her single friends, talking, conversing, consulting them for words of wisdom and heeding to their advice.

This detrimental attitude of reaching out to her single friends and including them in her marital experiences became a part of her lifestyle. As any wise person would predict, she eventually began encountering issues in her

marriage without knowing the cause. Unbeknown to her, she was not getting the best out of marriage because she kept seeking advice from her single friends.

These were people who had never been married, never kept healthy relationships with the opposite sex and some did not even share the same faith with her. It was obvious that because of their position in life they were not the best candidates to provide good counsel to her in that regard.

It is amazing how we often assume that those who were with us in the past automatically qualify to go where we are going (future). The bricks of the past should not be used to build the foundation on which the future will stand and therefore cannot be used as accompanying materials to build the future.

The friends she had were from her past and should have been limited on how much influence she gave to them concerning her marriage. Moreover, knowing that the heart of man is desperately wicked according to

Jeremiah 17:9, they could even be jealous or envious of her marriage and purposely leading her down the wrong path.

Rhonda could not enjoy the blessing she had right in front of her. She was not aware of the havoc that she was causing herself as a result of her ignorance. God moved her into a palace with the man of her dreams but she continued to look back at her past and what was behind her instead of looking forward.

She was physically married to her husband but mentally glued to the friends of her past; she was mentally married to her single life which would eventually affect her marriage. Many people have suffered from this same thing which has caused them to end up in a terrible divorce or one unpleasant place or the other.

Rhonda's dilemma illustrates why many people struggle with prosperity in life. God has called us as His children out of darkness into His kingdom of marvelous light but many are mentally stuck in darkness.

Instead of enjoying the benefits of the Kingdom of God, we look back to the things we are familiar with and know; just like Rhonda, not enjoying the full benefits of her marriage due to ignorance.

Another example of this form of ignorance can be found in Genesis 19. In short summary, God revealed His plan to destroy the city of Sodom and Gomorrah to Abraham. Upon hearing this, Abraham successfully negotiated with God to save the life of Lot (his nephew) and Lot's relatives. God sent two angels to rescue Lot and his family members.

After they were safely escorted out of the city, the angel of God warned, "Run for your lives! And don't look back or stop anywhere in the valley! Escape to the mountains, or you will be swept away! (Genesis 19:17)." Unfortunately, Lot's wife **looked back** and was turned into a pillar of salt. She was blessed with the opportunity of starting afresh but her mind was still in the city of Sodom. Unfortunately, the price for her ignorance was her life.

Ignorance Can Cause You To Miss Opportunities

This is one reason why the Word of God declares that we should not be conformed to this world but be transformed by the renewal of our minds (Romans 12:2). In ignorance, we are unable to enjoy the full benefits of operating in God's kingdom as His children.

Additionally, ignorance will cause one to miss numerous blessings and great opportunities and may even result in death on many levels. It is therefore imperative that every mountain of ignorance be removed from our path. It is my prayer that God will deliver you from every strong hold of ignorance in Jesus' Name!!!

Prayers from Chapter Five

Scripture: 2 Peter 3:8 But, beloved, be not ignorant of this one thing, that one day *is* with the Lord as a thousand years, and a thousand years as one day.

Prayer Points:

1. Father, let every stronghold of ignorance be destroyed by the anointing of the Holy Ghost in Jesus' Name.

2. Holy Spirit please do not leave me uninformed concerning things about my future.

3. Father, please reveal every hidden purpose inside of me, to me, in Jesus' Name.

4. Father in Heaven, please help me make the right decisions today in Jesus' Name.

5. Holy Spirit, lead me to the right people and places in Jesus' Name.

6. Father in Heaven, please help me to identify the real me in you in Jesus' Name.

7. Father, cause your word to open the eyes of my understanding that I might not walk in ignorance anymore in Jesus' Name.

8. Now, I stand on the Word of God and I command every evil mountain of ignorance to be destroyed in Jesus' Name.

9. Father let anything that distracts me from the truth be removed in Jesus' Name.

10. I disconnect myself from anything negative that promotes ignorance in Jesus' Name.

CHAPTER SIX

DISOBEDIENCE

*YE SHALL OBSERVE TO DO
THEREFORE AS THE LORD YOUR GOD
HATH COMMANDED YOU: YE SHALL
NOT TURN ASIDE TO THE RIGHT
HAND OR TO THE LEFT. YE SHALL
WALK IN ALL THE WAYS WHICH THE
LORD YOUR GOD HATH COMMANDED
YOU, THAT YE MAY LIVE, AND THAT
IT MAY BE WELL WITH YOU, AND
THAT YE MAY PROLONG YOUR DAYS
IN THE LAND WHICH YE SHALL
POSSESS.*

DEUTERONOMY 5:32-33

The Lord Is Our Shepherd

Just like every good father, God wants the best for His Children but for us to receive these things, we have to first obey him. No good parent rewards a disobedient child. King David caught this revelation of obedience very early in his life in Psalm 23 when he said "the Lord is my shepherd, I shall not want."

As a shepherd boy, he reckoned the fact that for as long as the sheep is obedient to the shepherd, there will always be provision. This principle worked very well for him and many others in the Bible; the truth is that, many years down the line, IT STILL WORKS.

1 Samuel 15 tells the story of a disobedient king named Saul. The Lord had given King Saul specific instructions to go to war against the Amalekites and completely destroy the nation's inhabitants inclusive of all the livestock. King Saul spared the life of the king of the Amalekites as well as the best livestock **against the Lord's wishes**. When Prophet Samuel confronted King Saul about his disobedience,

Saul said that he spared the livestock in order to present them as a burnt offering to God. In response to the disobedient act of Saul, Prophet Samuel responded, What is more pleasing to the Lord: your burnt offerings and sacrifices or your obedience to his voice?

Listen! Obedience is better than sacrifice, and submission is better than offering the fat of rams. Rebellion is as sinful as witchcraft, and stubbornness as bad as worshiping idols. So because you have rejected the command of the Lord, he has rejected you as king (1Samuel 15:22-23, NLT)."

Essentially, God rejected Saul because of his disobedience. Partial obedience was seen as total disobedience. Saul's disobedience stripped him of the honor of being the king of Israel and the privileges that came with it. Even more terrifying was the fact that God regretted ever making Saul the King (see 1 Samuel 15:35).

Disobedience Brings Trouble In Life

Disobedience brings shame and dishonor. It brings to mind the story of a man who gave a lot (he was an emotional giver) but he did not pay his tithe. As a matter of fact, he was giving more than his tithe. But it was not until he was struck by a catastrophic calamity that it was brought to his attention by a Great Man of God, that the reason why he was going through what he was going through was, because he was not paying his tithe.

He was doing good but not doing what was right; he was sacrificing but not obeying. Like King Saul he was more focused on sacrificing than obeying. Upon reading the example of Saul, we can rightfully conclude that disobedience is a major hindrance to prosperity and could also potentially strip you of blessings you might have already acquired.

Being disobedient to God's instruction can cause your life to collapse deeply into the realm of poverty by preventing you from operating in

your rightful position as a blessed child of God. The choice to be obedient to God's instructions can mean the difference between living in prosperity or in poverty.

In Isaiah 1:19 we see a promise attached to obedience: "If ye be willing and obedient, ye shall eat the good of the land." This tells us that our obedience is one main key to partaking in the best that God has made available to us. "The good of the land," could be that career, spouse, good health, peace, success, ministry, or the many other things that you desire.

One major self-inflicted obstacle that could be preventing you from experiencing the manifestation of the Word of God concerning your life is your total obedience to God. In your obedience, God will rejoice over you and reward you as well; disobedience on the other hand will bring reproach. Another profound commandment that provides directions to prosperity is found in Joshua 1:8. It illustrates the benefit of walking in obedience, it says "this book of the law shall not depart out of thy

mouth; but thou shalt meditate therein day and night, that thou mayest observe to do according to all that is written therein: for then thou shalt make thy way prosperous, and then thou shalt have good success."

This scripture releases a major key to walking in prosperity. How does one obey God's commandments if they are oblivious to what God has asked them to do? It is impossible to obey God's word without reading and knowing what God requires. Reading and meditating on the word of God will literally lighten your path, ultimately leading you to the life of prosperity that God desires for you.

The scripture goes further to introduce a level of success and prosperity that is often not spoken about; Joshua talks about something called **GOOD SUCCESS** (then thou shalt have good success). God does not only want you to be prosperous and successful, He wants you to have success beyond imagination. What He calls GOOD SUCCESS. Are you ready for good success? It begins with OBEDIENCE.

It is important to understand that as children of God, we represent His kingdom here on Earth. God is Almighty. The earth is His, and the fullness thereof, including the whole world, and all that dwell therein (Psalm 24:1). EVERYTHING belongs to our Father in heaven. Since we are His representatives here on earth, everything we do should direct attention to Our Heavenly Father.

If your biological father is blessed and you are living in obedience to him, wherever you go, you will be recognized as the son/daughter of your father because your father's blessings will be apparent on you. In the middle-eastern and other cultures, children carry their father's name wherever they go.

In that same manner we carry the name of our Heavenly Father. In a typical middle-eastern culture, you can easily tell where someone is from or which family they belong to simply by their name (their father's name is often associated to theirs not only as a surname). You and I today carry a name that is

not our own name; we live on the borrowed name just like we live on borrowed life. In Genesis, you realize that it was the breath of God that made man a living soul and when we die that breath is taken away (borrowed life).

It Is Better To Just Obey God

In that same manner we carry His name, that is why we are called **children of God**. In 2 Chronicles 7:14, God makes it clear by saying "if my people who are **called by my name**, will humble themselves, and pray, and seek my face, and turn from their wicked ways; then will I hear from heaven, and will forgive their sin, and will heal their land." We are His People called by His Name. In Genesis 1:28 God commands us to be fruitful, multiply and prosper.

Since this is a command, we as believers are mandated to live up to this so as to bring honor to His name. God does not want His enemies to mock you in anyway; He wants you to live a fulfilled life according to His word. Claiming to

be a child of God and not walking in obedience will cause you to look like a hypocrite which displays a negative image and impression of what it means to be a born-again child of God.

As representatives of God, He wants others to see our great works, the light we carry and hence give glory to Him (Matthew 5:16); this is our responsibility as children of God. There is a level of success and blessing that no man or amount of education can give you. Sometimes it takes the mighty hand of God to bring this high level of success which is often ignited by total obedience to God.

At the beginning of this year, a young lady called me with a disheartening voice to ask me to stand with her in prayer because she had just lost her 100% educational scholarship and her current income was barely paying the bills.

Above all this, she had just purchased a brand new expensive truck and taken up other philanthropic expenses. In fact, I knew that the scholarship was really needed at the moment. After praying for her, I told her, "I believe God

will give you another scholarship opportunity."

Later in the year, I received a similar phone call from her. This time around, her job was being threatened. After, praying with her, I said, "you will get a better job opportunity but I want you to start your master's degree as well." However, it didn't make sense for someone in her situation to add more financial pressure by starting a master's degree.

After consistent frustration at her current job and an unsuccessful job search, she finally decided to go back to school to work on her MBA while looking for a better job. Approximately a month after commencing her MBA she met some great classmates who decided to actively help her with her job hunt. Through one of her classmates, she was offered a better job opportunity in a huge company. In addition to this, the company offered to pay her tuition in full (FULL SCHOLARSHIP!).

WHAT A DETAILED GOD WE SERVE! You see my friend, all this unraveled when she finally decided to be obedient to what she heard. God had already finished the work, the only thing that was

> How you respond to what you hear goes a long way to determine what you receive from what you hear.

missing was **her obedience.** How you respond to what you hear goes a long way to determine what you receive from what you hear. God has so much in stock for those who will diligently adhere to His voice; He has your best interest at heart.

He's got each detail figured out already, all you need to do is to obey. Being the fact that God has your best interest at heart, He has in fact given instructions and directions for your protection and long-term benefit so that you can prosper in every area of your life. On the other hand, being disobedient to God means you have rejected and turned your back against the direction of God which in itself is rebellion. Rebellion is a spirit that slowly kills.

Throughout scripture, we see the falling of many great men and women as a result of some sort of rebellion. When the spirit of rebellion takes over your life, you are doomed. It is a spirit that must actively be resisted; it often works hand in hand with pride.

Often times, those who are rebellious are also proud. Now that you know, look back at some scenarios that you might have heard of in the past and you will realize that this is absolutely true.

In the case of the story of Absalom and his father, King David, you realize that it was pride that led Absalom to become rebellious and this cost him his life (Read 2 Samuel 15, 16,17, & 18). Disobedience, which is a form of rebellion, kills.

The spirit of rebellion comes with knowledge; it feeds the minds of people with rebellious information. When that same spirit took over Judas, he was filled with the entire strategy(information) of betrayal concerning Jesus (Read Luke 22). Spirits therefore carry

information.

If evil spirits carry bad information, it is obvious the kind of information our Precious Holy Spirit carries. The spirit of God connects us to information (knowledge) that leads to our success. Without Him, we will be wandering around in circles and knocking on walls thinking they are doors. Simply put, without the knowledge, wisdom and understanding of the Holy Spirit, we will be complete failures.

In Isaiah 11:2 we read concerning Jesus Christ that "the Spirit of that Lord shall rest upon Him, the spirit of Wisdom and understanding, the spirit of counsel and might, the spirit of knowledge..." Even Jesus Christ needed this knowledge, wisdom and understanding provided by our Precious Holy Spirit to succeed in His life and ministry.

Our bodies are referred to as the temple of the Holy Ghost (Read 1 Corinthians 6:19). Therefore, when the Holy Ghost comes into the temple, our total submission to Him is needed for Him to be able to fully operate in our lives.

This involves maximum obedience. Refusing to obey God is simply saying no to the **benefits** that He brings us. One common factor among disobedient folks is that they are normally driven by the **lust of the flesh, lust of the eye** and **the pride of life**.

These factors of disobedience keep people in a cycle of stagnation, retrogression and a cycle of unwanted challenges in life. Disobeying God is another way of saying, "I don't need God." Nothing good can come out of disobedience. Disobedience has many consequences that even this small book cannot contain. Disobedience is the number one hindrance of prosperity, good success, good health, peace, joy and many more. God is a God of principles and disobeying His principles will definitely cause you to forfeit the benefits of those principles.

There is a man who is written about in the Bible, his name is Jonah (Read Jonah 1,2,3,4). He was given instructions by God to deliver a message of repentance to the city of Nineveh.

> God is a God of principles and disobeying His principles will definitely cause you to forfeit the benefits of those principles.

However, he tried to avoid this assignment by moving in the opposite direction God told him to go. Instead of heading to Nineveh, he got onto a ship and headed to Tarshish. **He was being disobedient.** God sent a mighty wind into the sea creating a great storm. The storm was so bad and devastating that the sailors were afraid and began to encourage each other to pray for their lives.

They recognized that Jonah was asleep and told him to pray to His God. Anxious to know if anyone was the cause for the problem they began to cast lots and in doing so they identified Jonah as the problem. They threw him overboard and immediately, the storm

stopped. He was swallowed by a great fish and he remained there for three days and three nights.

It was during this time that Jonah decided to pray and the Lord heard his cry. *"And said, I cried by reason of mine affliction unto the LORD, and he heard me; out of the belly of hell cried I, and thou heardest my voice, Jonah 2:2."* Eventually Jonah repented and did as God commanded. Many often think that disobedience is normally a result of what one did or did not do; however, it also includes our thought life and our silent conceptions (the inside).

One of the significant points in the book of Jonah is that the boat was attacked not because of the captain or anyone else but because of Jonah's disobedience to God (an insider). For this reason, God chose the winds to attack the ship. When you are disobedient and moving outside of the will and direction of God, you are liable to experience many different types of storms.

On the ship that Jonah boarded, there were many people who were all affected by the storms. These were innocent people; HOW SAD. They were affected as a result of one man's disobedience. It reminds me of Lamentations 5:7(NLT) where the people cried out to God saying "*our ancestors sinned, but they have died and we are suffering the punishment they deserve.*" Many people have suffered many undeserving things as a result of another person's disobedience.

From the story of Jonah, we can deduce that your blessing could be hindered as a result of someone else's disobedience. In other words, you could even suffer a lack of manifestation in your life just by being on the same ship with a disobedient person. **Wow, this is serious!**

Just as disobedience can cause your boat to sink, obedience can cause your boat to rise and sail smoothly. The same water that can cause you to drown can cause you to rise and sail peacefully. Being obedient to the instructions of God brings direction to your life and favor

with God. Obedience to God and submitting to the leading of Our Precious Holy Spirit will lead you to the right places and the right people.

True Prosperity commences with obedience. Despite praying, seeking God's favor, and acting "righteous," you will not see any manifestation by walking in disobedience. Jeremiah 29:11 reveals *"For I know the thoughts that I think toward you, saith the LORD, thoughts of peace, and not of evil, to give you an expected end."*

God wants to give you an expected end, an end of success and victory. If you cannot live in obedience, the expected end that God has envisioned for you might not manifest. God really wants to do "exceedingly and abundantly above all you can ask or think" in your life but the decision to accept this is in your obedience.

Beloved, you have a choice to make. The plans of God for you are obviously good but the choice of whether you will accept it or not is in your hands. The book of Joshua 24:14 can sum it all up: *" 14Now therefore fear the LORD, and*

serve him in sincerity and in truth: and put away the gods which your fathers served on the other side of the flood, and in Egypt; and serve ye the LORD. [15] And if it seem evil unto you to serve the LORD, choose you this day whom ye will serve; whether the gods which your fathers served that were on the other side of the flood, or the gods of the Amorites, in whose land ye dwell: but as for me and my house, we will serve the LORD."

Prayers from Chapter Six

Scripture: Isaiah 1:18-19   [18]Come now, and let us reason together, saith the LORD: though your sins be as scarlet, they shall be as white as snow; though they be red like crimson, they shall be as wool. [19]If ye be willing and obedient, ye shall eat the good of the land:

Prayer Points:

1. Father, I submit myself to your will and boldly declare that from this day forward I am free from the operation of every spirit of disobedience.

2. I denounce the power of every spirit of disobedience in my life in Jesus' Name.

3. I declare that I am free from every stronghold of disobedience in Jesus' Name.

4. I divorce every spirit of pride in the Name of Jesus.

5. I renounce my connection with disobedient people in Jesus' Name.

6. Father in Heaven lead me on the right path according to Psalms 23 in Jesus' Name.

7. Father in Heaven, let your precious Holy Spirit guide me into the right places and to the right people at the right time in Jesus' Name.

8. Father, may my ways not bring you displeasure as a result of disobedience but rather, let my ways bring you happiness in Jesus' Name.

9. Father, make me an example of the benefits of obedience in Jesus' Name.

10. Now I stand in the authority of the word of God and I bind every Spirit of rebellion that is active in my life in Jesus' Name.

11. I announce the divorce of every Spirit of Rebellion operating in my life in Jesus' Name.

12. I renounce the Spirit of Pride.

13. I declare that I am free from the oppression of the Spirit of Rebellion in Jesus' Name.

14. I declare that I will not be led into the wrong ship in Jesus' Name.

15. From this day forward, not only am I filled with Our Precious Holy Ghost but I declare that I fully belong to Him and am therefore fully led by Him in Jesus' Name.

CHAPTER SEVEN

LAZINESS

24 THE HAND OF THE DILIGENT SHALL BEAR RULE: BUT THE SLOTHFUL SHALL BE UNDER TRIBUTE.

PROVERBS 12:24

In the book of Matthew 25:14-30, Jesus tells us the story of a man who entrusted his money to his three servants before going on a long trip. He gave the money to each of them according to their abilities.

The first servant was given five pieces of silver, the second servant was given two pieces of silver, and the last servant was given one piece of silver. Upon his return, he was pleased to find that the servant given the five pieces of silver produced five more, and the servant that was given the two pieces of silver produced two more.

Unfortunately, the servant that was given one piece of silver could not multiply or make any additions to it. His master called him a "wicked" and "lazy" servant because he did not utilize what was entrusted to him. Many people today are like the man who was given only one talent (piece) of silver. As a matter of fact, many people die without even knowing the gifts and talents given to them.

Everything needed for a bird to survive is

placed in the bird when it is born, this same principle applies to lions, dogs and every animal that you can think about. If that is the case, don't you think that God has already placed in you all that is needed to make you successful? When He created you, all your needs were provided.

You see, God has entrusted you with the necessary tools to be prosperous in life. There are gifts inside of you; there is silver and gold in you, what you do with it determines what you get out of it. What are you doing with the "silver" God has given you? Out of laziness, many people deliberately neglect these gifts on the inside for many different reasons (excuses).

God wants us to be good stewards of the gifts and attributes He has deposited in us. On the flip side of the coin, a part of the enemy's desire is to hinder you from coming to knowledge of these gifts deposited in you. If the enemy fails at this, he then tries to distract you from putting those talents to work with many different things to include "laziness." Laziness

is not a friend of success; it is an enemy of success.

Laziness is defined as "the quality of being unwilling to work or use energy; idleness." Laziness is an attribute that prevents one from attaining success and prosperity while simultaneously opening the door to poverty. The wisest King of his time said in Proverbs 6:10-11 that "A little sleep, a little slumber, a little folding of the hands to rest— and poverty will come on you like a thief and scarcity like an armed man."

Laziness Brings Poverty

Laziness can be identified in an individual who lacks the drive or motivation to improve mentally, physically, educationally, and spiritually. People of this nature are often led by how they feel; now, you need to understand that the body, most likely will always mislead you to make the wrong decision.

It is therefore important to always remind yourself **that there is tremendous reward in hard work**. Hard work is a common trait among all successful people who continue

> Hard work will not only get you there, it will keep you there.

to remain successful. Hard work will not only get you there, it will keep you there.

I believe that folks can be bound by laziness. Some traits of these people include their weird desire to remain stagnant in life, blaming others for past failures, choosing to doubt the vision that God first gave them, oversleeping, procrastinating, always seeing the worst in opportunities, shying away from successful people, being unwilling to undertake new ventures and the list goes on and on.

These characteristics and attributes prevent success and provide a foothold for poverty. It is like sending a special invitation to poverty. One thing that is known about poverty is that it is more quick to show up than success.

The comfort that comes with laziness is

temporary but the consequences are often very brutal. The subject of laziness is so detrimental to the extent that King Solomon repeats the exact same words in Proverbs 6:10-11 and Proverbs 24:33-34; that is how serious it is.

Mind you, King Solomon was the wisest man in his time and therefore did not lack words of wisdom to avoid repeating the same thing in the same book (the book of Proverbs).

If you have ever watched the news, you know that victims of armed robbery are often left wounded physically, traumatized emotionally, and stripped of their possessions.

King Solomon said *"poverty will come on you like a thief and scarcity like an armed man";* this means that an individual could potentially open the door to all these attacks in their life spiritually and physically just by simply being lazy.

Yes, the enemy can come in like an armed robber if you let him in through laziness. There are numerous accounts of wasted potential and talents due to laziness. Unfortunately, it does

not stop there.

As laziness and poverty are intertwined, an entire generation can be cursed with the spirit of poverty due to the laziness of one individual. As you can see, you are an important factor in your generation; **YOU MATTER**. You can either perpetuate the cycle of laziness and poverty or be the force that brings that curse to an end, which will positively impact numerous generations after you.

If you desire God to use you in any capacity, start working hard in your daily activities. Approach every assignment given to you with exuberance, zeal, and enthusiasm. Look for opportunities to grow, excel, and improve.

> Dare to do and become the extraordinary!

Always seek to improve on yourself; never settle for the ordinary but rather, dare to do and become the extraordinary. You have what it takes; you can make it! Believe in yourself!

When Jesus (the one who came to teach us how to live right) was on the earth, He

surrounded Himself with hard working individuals; the most successful tax collectors, fishermen and the Peters - those who tried, failed and got back up to try again (very resilient people).

This goes a long way to attest to the fact that when you are hard-working, you stand a chance to be used by God. God is looking for men and women who are not physically and/or spiritually lazy with their gift and are willing to go the extra mile for His kingdom and for themselves.

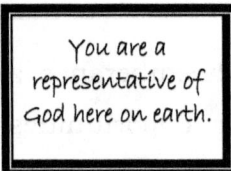

You need to understand that you are a representative of God here on earth and as His representative, you make Him look good when you increase in productivity. In fact Jesus said in Matthew 5:16 to "let your light so shine before men, that they may see your good works, and glorify your Father which is in heaven."

> You are a representative of God here on earth.

In today's society, many people find themselves doing things that are not related to

their purpose on the earth. It is understandable that the vicissitudes of this life often demands that you pursue provision instead of purpose. However, this should not be a show stopper for you. Let me share a very significant example that occurred in scripture with you.

John 21:3-6(HCSB) says *"I'm going fishing," Simon Peter said to them. "We're coming with you," they told him. They went out and got into the boat, but that night they caught nothing.⁴ When daybreak came, Jesus stood on the shore. However, the disciples did not know it was Jesus.⁵ "Men,"[a] Jesus called to them, "you don't have any fish, do you?" "No," they answered. ⁶ "Cast the net on the right side of the boat," He told them, "and you'll find some." So they did,[b] and they were unable to haul it in because of the large number of fish."*

Wow, what a powerful lesson. They knew what their purpose was but they were driven by the vicissitudes of life to pursue "provision" (fishing) instead of "purpose" (preaching the gospel). As a result of neglecting their purpose,

they toiled all night without catching any fish (provision).

The good news is that when they finally identified the voice of Jesus Christ (the voice of purpose), their problem (provision) was solved. You might have neglected your purpose for some time now but it is never too late to go back to "purpose fulfillment"; Jesus (the voice of purpose) is calling you to start that business, ministry, education, career, marriage etc., listen to His Voice and stop worrying about provision.

> Provision is the number one hindrance to purpose.

Provision is the number one hindrance to purpose.

Purpose, just like anything else, cannot be pursued without adequate motivation. Lack of motivation to take the extra step necessary to manifest dreams, visions and goals in life is also a great hindrance perpetuated by the enemy through laziness. Lazy people often lack motivation to do any good thing. The most common excuse given is

that they are working a full-time job and therefore are unable to pursue those goals.

Be Diligent

In Acts 20:34, Paul talks about working with his hands in order to supply his needs and the needs of his

> Laziness is an enemy of success.

companions. If the forerunners in the Bible were able to work and also pursue their passions, we have no excuse. Working a full-time job is not an excuse for you to give up on the dreams and talents God has given to you. If you find yourself in that position, my suggestion is that you keep your full-time job and start using that God given talent as a side business or commitment.

It might take a little extra sacrifice like waking up earlier than normal, going to sleep later than normal, giving up some meals, giving up some of your favorite TV programs and many more. The good news is that as you continue to pursue purpose in this manner, with prayer and hard work, God will eventually

lead you to the desired place.

I have seen many people who have applied this method until their purpose replaced their full-time Job. My friend, there is so much joy in pursuing purpose; don't allow laziness to stop you:

➤ Laziness causes retrogression in life
➤ Laziness is a spirit/trap
➤ Laziness is one of the worst cancers in life
➤ Laziness is an evil seed that has the potency to become a well rooted stronghold in one's life
➤ Laziness involves an ungodly relationship
➤ Laziness will always lead to your demise
➤ Laziness is an enemy of progress
➤ Laziness brings misery
➤ Laziness comforts misery

Prayers from Chapter Seven

Scripture: Proverbs 10:4 "A slack hand causes poverty, but the hand of the diligent makes rich."

Prayer Points:

1. Father in Heaven, please help me to be able to pursue your purpose for my life in Jesus' Name.

2. Father, please bless my hands to be diligent; may they never slack.

3. Father please give me the strength to overcome any form of laziness in my life in Jesus' Name.

4. I stand on the Word of God and declare that I am rising to my place of purpose fulfilment in Jesus' Name.

5. Father, I submit myself to you and I ask that you release me from every bondage of laziness.

6. I stand on the Word of God and I declare that every cycle of Laziness is broken in Jesus' Name.

7. I disconnect myself from every association of laziness in Jesus' Name.

8. I stand on the Word of God and I bind every spirit of laziness operating in my life in Jesus' name!

9. I command every trap of laziness to be destroyed by fire in Jesus' name!

10. I resist the operation of every evil spirit of laziness in my life in Jesus' Name.

11. I cancel every assignment of the enemy to stagnate my growth in Jesus' Name.

12. I cancel every assignment of the enemy to stagnate my assignment in Jesus' Name.

13. I declare that my life will not remain stagnant in Jesus' Name.

14. I declare that the spirit of stagnation associated with the spirit of laziness has

no hold in my life any longer in Jesus' Name!

15. I uproot any seed of laziness planted in my life in Jesus' name!

16. Father, let every stronghold of laziness operating in my life and family be broken in Jesus' name!

17. I disconnect myself from the ties of laziness in the name of Jesus.

18. I disconnect myself from any ungodly relationship with laziness in Jesus' name!

19. I declare that my life is free from misery in Jesus' name!

20. I decree and declare that my life will not be infected by the miserable. consequences of laziness in Jesus' name!

21. From this day onward, I declare that no spirit of laziness shall be able to operate in my family in Jesus' Name.

22. I declare my liberty and the liberty of my family from any power of laziness in Jesus' Name.

CHAPTER EIGHT

BECOMING BETTER!

¹⁰YET A LITTLE SLEEP, A LITTLE
SLUMBER, A LITTLE FOLDING OF THE
HANDS TO SLEEP: ¹¹SO SHALL THY
POVERTY COME AS ONE THAT
TRAVELLETH, AND THY WANT AS AN
ARMED MAN.

PROVERBS 6:10-11

It is written in Galatians 3:26 that we are all Children of God by faith in Christ Jesus. As a result of this, we are co heirs with Christ and our bodies are the members of Christ (Read 1 Corinthians 6:15). Part of this means that we have inherited every spiritual and physical possession that Jesus had access to while on the earth and in heaven.

In other words, the moment you received Jesus as your Lord and Personal Savior, you were given access to the keys that unlock the inherited blessings stored up for you through Christ Jesus. Prosperity was a major part of the inheritance that Jesus Christ exhibited a lot throughout His ministry. Due to the fact that Jesus Christ came to teach us how to live, I am thoroughly convinced that God wants us to live a prosperous life like Jesus did. 1 John 2:6(NIV) says "*Whoever claims to live in him must live as Jesus did*"; what a powerful statement.

As an example, Jesus' official ministry began at thirty years old and within a short span of time, He had prospered to the point that His

impact was felt and talked about across that region. As a matter of fact we are still seeing the impact of His ministry in our lives today; it is still prospering.

If Jesus was able to be prosperous while on the earth, we only have to examine His life and emulate his actions in order to see those same results in our lives. Therefore, we as Children of God, have no obligation to be bound by the things that causes us to live a life less than what He wants us to live.

An important scripture that sums up God's expectations for us is found in *Romans 8:1-8:* "*1There is therefore now no condemnation to them which are in Christ Jesus, who walk not after the flesh, but after the Spirit.2 For the law of the Spirit of life in Christ Jesus hath made me free from the law of sin and death.3For what the law could not do, in that it was weak through the flesh, God sending his own Son in the likeness of sinful flesh, and for sin, condemned sin in the flesh:4That the righteousness of the law might be fulfilled in us, who walk not after*

the flesh, but after the Spirit. [5]For they that are after the flesh do mind the things of the flesh; but they that are after the Spirit the things of the Spirit. [6] For to be carnally minded is death; but to be spiritually minded is life and peace. [7]Because the carnal mind is enmity against God: for it is not subject to the law of God, neither indeed can be. [8]So then they that are in the flesh cannot please God. It is not God's will for His children to live in ignorance of who God has made them to be and the **treasures at their reach**."

You Are A Royal Priesthood

What benefit is it for a slave to have obtained his or her freedom, come into a wealthy inheritance and yet have no clue about it? The same goes for you, my friend. Through Jesus Christ, we have obtained victory, freedom and authority but many of us remain bound by the stronghold of ignorance. **THIS IS AN ERROR.** How can we possess something we have no knowledge about?

It is therefore very important to study and meditate on the Manual (the Word) given to us

by the Manufacturer (God). This will then bring us to a full knowledge of who we truly are in Him and also the spiritual inheritance available to us as the children of God. Whatever happens, do not miss out on your own inheritance.

For our protection, God has given us directions to walk in the fruit of the spirit. The fruit of the Spirit is love, joy, peace, longsuffering, gentleness, goodness, faith, meekness and temperance (Galatians 5:22-23). When we leave doors of the flesh open to Satan, he gains an advantage over us.

Give The Enemy No Place

Doors that entice Satan are the ones that create mental slavery and strongholds. These doors can include fear, shame, regrets, anger, un-forgiveness, strife, hate, shame, jealousy, resentment, wrath, factions, rebellion, division, envy, and lying. These are attributes that will hinder your prosperity, deprive your life and bring internal distress.

Satan's ultimate goal has never changed from the beginning. He influenced Adam to disobey by eating from the forbidden tree. This disobedience led to an outcome of sin and death. In John 10:10 Jesus states that *"The thief cometh not, but for to steal, and to kill, and to destroy: I am come that they might have life, and that they might have it more abundantly."* This has always been his goal.

Although we as believers have been redeemed from Adam's sin through Jesus Christ, Satan still ignites great motivation to sin. He does everything possible to keep us separated from God by influencing us to disobey; just as he did to Adam.

When we perpetuate a lifestyle of disobedience, our prayers are no longer effective and we lose our candidacy for complete prosperity. This is why we must endeavor to repent(change our minds). Along with repentance, we must seek to please God through our everyday activities.

Although our desire is to live prosperous

lives, our ultimate goal should be to please God in what we think, say, and do. As this desire to please God increases, we will do that which is good and shun that which is evil. The by-product of this mindset is prosperity in all areas of our life.

A vital aspect of desiring to please God is ensuring that everything concerning your life lines up with God's Word and God's will for your life. This means keeping Him at the forefront of your mind whether at work, school, or completing your daily activities. This, coupled with earnest prayer, will position you for increased prosperity in your life.

God is a rewarder of those who sincerely seek Him (Hebrews 11:6). It is therefore very important to become intentional about eliminating any behavior that would interfere with being in God's presence and living in prosperity.

I always say that if John the revelator was not in the Spirit on the Lord's Day, He probably would not have received the book of revelation

(*Revelation 1:10 NIV, On the Lord's Day I was in the Spirit, and I heard behind me a loud voice like a trumpet*). It is indeed very important to intentionally live in a way that is pleasing to God.

I encourage you to allow the power of God to restore and heal you so that you may stand and operate effectively in His Kingdom. In life, we make mistakes but we are not mandated to repeat the same mistakes although that is often the goal of the wicked one.

You have what it takes to do things right and get the best that God wants you to get. You have what it takes to reject the enemy called poverty. I declare that every cycle of failure in your life breaks today in Jesus' Name!!!

Prayers from Chapter Eight

Scripture: Proverbs 10:22

22 The blessing of the Lord, it maketh rich, and he addeth no sorrow with it.

Prayer Points:

1. Father in Heaven, according to your word, remove every area of lack, insufficiency and depravation out of my life and let there be an overflow of blessings that make me rich: mentally, emotionally, spiritually, physically financially and in relationships and adds no sorrow.

2. Father in Heaven, according to your word, I ask that you release the anointing to make wealth come upon me in Jesus' Name.

3. Let the anointing to make wealth locate me in Jesus' Name.

4. Make me an exhibition of your wealth in Jesus' Name.

5. I declare that I am blessed and highly favored in Jesus' Name.

6. I renounce every element of Poverty in my life in Jesus' Name.

7. Let every error of Poverty in my life be corrected in Jesus' Name.

8. I renounce any form of anger in Jesus' Name.

9. I renounce any form of strife in Jesus' Name.

10. I renounce any form of hate in my life and around me in Jesus' Name.

11. I renounce any form of jealousy and resentment in Jesus' Name.

12. I renounce any spirit of rebellion in Jesus' Name.

13. I come against every attack of division in Jesus' Name.

14. I block the operation of any lying spirit in my life, my family and my surroundings in Jesus' Name.

15. Father in Heaven, let the fruit of the spirit be exhibited in my life in its entirety in Jesus' Name.

CHAPTER NINE

CONCLUSION

THERE IS A WAY WHICH SEEMETH
RIGHT UNTO A MAN, BUT THE END
THEREOF ARE THE WAYS OF DEATH.
PROVERBS 14:12

God (our manufacturer) wants us to live life in an abundant and joyful way but this can only happen if we follow the instructions of His manual (His Word). His ways of doing things are very different from the way we do things as mortal men and women.

He stated clearly in Isaiah 55:9 that "As the heavens are higher than the earth, so are my ways higher than your ways and my thoughts than your thoughts." As humans it is almost a norm to take our lives in our own hands instead of depending fully on God.

I remember, growing up as a child, my mother would always say "what an adult sees while sitting on the floor cannot be seen by a child standing on a chair." This paradox is a description of the insight that adults have which children often do not have.

Adults often see years ahead of time while kids only see and think about "now." It is similar to what King Solomon said in Proverbs 14:12, *"there is a way that seemeth right unto man."*

Growing up as a child, there were many things that I wanted to do and have. Although I was told that it was not good for me, I still wanted it. The problem is that I did not understand the consequences of having those things and when the consequences were explained to me, I still wanted it due to my stubbornness at that time.

All I needed to do was to listen to my parents and trust that they would not lead me to a place that was not good for me. It sounds simple now but it was not easy for me to understand at that time. My way of thinking was very narrow; I wanted my own way.

At times, I did not even trust the promises and directions the adults gave me. Looking back now, I realize that all I needed to do was to trust their leading and everything else would have fallen in place.

In that same way, God wants us to trust Him and His process. He wants us to live by His Word which will eventually lead us to where He wants us to get to. He does not want us to be

myopic in spiritual sight but instead, He wants us to see things like He sees things.

Although you might not understand some of the instructions given in scripture, it is very important that you trust God at His Word because it will bring you to an expected end. A very powerful man came to Jesus and expressed His understanding of the Power of the Word of God. This was a man who had even built a synagogue for that nation (Read Luke 7:5). Yet, he would not even let Jesus come to his house to pray for his sick servant because he did not count himself worthy. He said to Jesus "just say the word from where you are and my servant will be healed (Luke 7:7 AMP)."

Despite his accomplishment in the Nation and his wealth, he did not require Jesus to do for him what many would require. He understood that if he could just get a "Word" of healing from Jesus, his servant would be healed.

This is the kind of faith God wants us to have in His Word. He wants us to have crazy faith.

Crazy faith in God will reveal a better "you" in Him. The truth is that almost everything about God takes faith. You have heard how it is written that without faith, it is impossible to please God (Read Hebrews 11:6).

God said in Jeremiah 29:11 *"For I know the plans I have for you," declares the L*ORD*, "plans to prosper you and not to harm you, plans to give you hope and a future."* We do not know the exact plans of

God for us but we do know for a fact that His plans for us are good and prosperous. Like the Centurion Man in Luke 7, it is my prayer that you will have faith enough to believe in His Word (written Word). You might not see the end but only believe. As you keep believing, you will realize at the end that you will finally become a better "You" in Him.

NOTES & REFLECTIONS

VINCENT KPODO

SCRIPTURES

THEN SAID JESUS TO THOSE JEWS
WHICH BELIEVED ON HIM, IF YE
CONTINUE IN MY WORD, THEN ARE
YE MY DISCIPLES INDEED; AND YE
SHALL KNOW THE TRUTH, AND THE
TRUTH SHALL MAKE YOU FREE.

JOHN 8 31-32

How We Should Treat Others:

Ephesians 4:32 - And be ye kind one to another, tenderhearted, forgiving one another, even as God for Christ's sake hath forgiven you.

Ephesians 4:29 - Let no corrupt communication proceed out of your mouth, but that which is good to the use of edifying, that it may minister grace unto the hearers.

John 15:12 - This is my commandment, That ye love one another, as I have loved you.

Luke 6:31 - And as ye would that men should do to you, do ye also to them likewise.

1 John 4:20 - If a man say, I love God, and hateth his brother, he is a liar: for he that loveth not his brother whom he hath seen, how

can he love God whom he hath not seen?

Proverbs 24:17 - Rejoice not when thine enemy falleth, and let not thine heart be glad when he stumbleth:

Matthew 7:12 - Therefore all things whatsoever ye would that men should do to you, do ye even so to them: for this is the law and the prophets.

Romans 15:1 - We then that are strong ought to bear the infirmities of the weak, and not to please ourselves.

Romans 12:10 - [Be] kindly affectioned one to another with brotherly love; in honour preferring one another;

1 Peter 3:8-12 - Finally, [be ye] all of one mind, having compassion one of another, love as

brethren, [be] pitiful, [be] courteous: [9] Not rendering evil for evil, or railing for railing: but contrariwise blessing; knowing that ye are thereunto called, that ye should inherit a blessing. [10] For he that will love life, and see good days, let him refrain his tongue from evil, and his lips that they speak no guile: [11] Let him eschew evil, and do good; let him seek peace, and ensue it. [12] For the eyes of the Lord are over the righteous, and his ears are open unto their prayers: but the face of the Lord is against them that do evil.

Philippians 2:4 - Look not every man on his own things, but every man also on the things of others.

Colossians 3:12-14 - Put on therefore, as the elect of God, holy and beloved, bowels of mercies, kindness, humbleness of mind, meekness, longsuffering; [13] Forbearing one another, and forgiving one another, if any man

have a quarrel against any: even as Christ forgave you, so also do ye. [14] And above all these things put on charity, which is the bond of perfectness.

James 2:1 - My brethren, have not the faith of our Lord Jesus Christ, [the Lord] of glory, with respect of persons.

Romans 12:18 - If it be possible, as much as lieth in you, live peaceably with all men.

Matthew 6:14 - For if ye forgive men their trespasses, your heavenly Father will also forgive you:

1 Peter 2:17 - Honour all [men]. Love the brotherhood. Fear God. Honour the king.

1 Corinthians 13:4 - Charity suffereth long, [and] is kind; charity envieth not; charity

vaunteth not itself, is not puffed up,

1 Timothy 5:1-2 - Rebuke not an elder, but intreat [him] as a father; [and] the younger men as brethren; [2] The elder women as mothers; the younger as sisters, with all purity.

Prosperity:

Deuteronomy 8:18 - But thou shalt remember the LORD thy God: for [it is] he that giveth thee power to get wealth, that he may establish his covenant which he sware unto thy fathers, as [it is] this day.

Jeremiah 29:11 - For I know the thoughts that I think toward you, saith the LORD, thoughts of peace, and not of evil, to give you an expected end.

Philippians 4:19 - But my God shall supply all your need according to his riches in glory by Christ Jesus.

Malachi 3:10 - Bring ye all the tithes into the storehouse, that there may be meat in mine house, and prove me now herewith, saith the LORD of hosts, if I will not open you the windows of heaven, and pour you out a blessing, that [there shall] not [be room] enough [to receive it].

3 John 1:2 - Beloved, I wish above all things that thou mayest prosper and be in health, even as thy soul prospereth.

Psalms 128:2 - For thou shalt eat the labour of thine hands: happy [shalt] thou [be], and [it shall be] well with thee.

Philippians 4:6 - Be careful for nothing; but in everything by prayer and supplication with thanksgiving let your requests be made known unto God.

Psalms 37:4 - Delight thyself also in the LORD; and he shall give thee the desires of thine heart.

Romans 8:28 - And we know that all things work together for good to them that love God, to them who are the called according to [his] purpose.

2 Peter 1:4 - Whereby are given unto us exceeding great and precious promises: that by these ye might be partakers of the divine nature, having escaped the corruption that is in the world through lust.

2 Corinthians 1:20 - For all the promises of God in him [are] yea, and in him Amen, unto the glory of God by us.

John 15:7 - If ye abide in me, and my words

abide in you, ye shall ask what ye will, and it shall be done unto you.

John 3:16 - For God so loved the world, that he gave his only begotten Son, that whosoever believeth in him should not perish, but have everlasting life.

Psalms 23:1 - (A Psalm of David.) The LORD [is] my shepherd; I shall not want.

2 Corinthians 9:8 - And God [is] able to make all grace abound toward you; that ye, always having all sufficiency in all [things], may abound to every good work:

Psalms 1:3 - And he shall be like a tree planted by the rivers of water, that bringeth forth his fruit in his season; his leaf also shall not wither; and whatsoever he doeth shall prosper.

2 Corinthians 8:9 - For ye know the grace of our Lord Jesus Christ, that, though he was rich, yet for your sakes he became poor, that ye through his poverty might be rich.

Proverbs 28:25 - He that is of a proud heart stirreth up strife: but he that putteth his trust in the LORD shall be made fat.

Zechariah 9:12 - Turn you to the strong hold, ye prisoners of hope: even today do I declare [that] I will render double unto thee;

Job 22:23 - If thou return to the Almighty, thou shalt be built up, thou shalt put away iniquity far from thy tabernacles.

Luke 6:38 - Give, and it shall be given unto you; good measure, pressed down, and shaken together, and running over, shall men give into your bosom. For with the same measure that

ye mete withal it shall be measured to you again.

Psalms 1:1-6 - Blessed [is] the man that walketh not in the counsel of the ungodly, nor standeth in the way of sinners, nor sitteth in the seat of the scornful.

Deuteronomy 28:1-14 - And it shall come to pass, if thou shalt hearken diligently unto the voice of the LORD thy God, to observe [and] to do all his commandments which I command thee this day, that the LORD thy God will set thee on high above all nations of the earth: [2] And all these blessings shall come on thee, and overtake thee, if thou shalt hearken unto the voice of the Lord thy God. [3] Blessed shalt thou be in the city, and blessed shalt thou be in the field. [4] Blessed shall be the fruit of thy body, and the fruit of thy ground, and the fruit of thy cattle, the increase of thy kine, and the flocks of thy sheep. [5] Blessed shall be thy basket

and thy store.[6] Blessed shalt thou be when thou comest in, and blessed shalt thou be when thou goest out.[7] The Lord shall cause thine enemies that rise up against thee to be smitten before thy face: they shall come out against thee one way, and flee before thee seven ways.[8] The Lord shall command the blessing upon thee in thy storehouses, and in all that thou settest thine hand unto; and he shall bless thee in the land which the Lord thy God giveth thee.[9] The Lord shall establish thee an holy people unto himself, as he hath sworn unto thee, if thou shalt keep the commandments of the Lord thy God, and walk in his ways.[10] And all people of the earth shall see that thou art called by the name of the Lord; and they shall be afraid of thee.[11] And the Lord shall make thee plenteous in goods, in the fruit of thy body, and in the fruit of thy cattle, and in the fruit of thy ground, in the land which the Lord sware unto thy fathers to give thee.[12] The Lord shall open unto thee his good treasure, the heaven to give the rain unto thy

land in his season, and to bless all the work of thine hand: and thou shalt lend unto many nations, and thou shalt not borrow. [13] And the Lord shall make thee the head, and not the tail; and thou shalt be above only, and thou shalt not be beneath; if that thou hearken unto the commandments of the Lord thy God, which I command thee this day, to observe and to do them: [14] And thou shalt not go aside from any of the words which I command thee this day, to the right hand, or to the left, to go after other gods to serve them.

Nehemiah 2:20 - Then answered I them, and said unto them, The God of heaven, he will prosper us; therefore we his servants will arise and build: but ye have no portion, nor right, nor memorial, in Jerusalem.

Obedience:

John 14:15 - If ye love me, keep my commandments.

Luke 6:46 - And why call ye me, Lord, Lord, and do not the things which I say?

Romans 6:16 - Know ye not, that to whom ye yield yourselves servants to obey, his servants ye are to whom ye obey; whether of sin unto death, or of obedience unto righteousness?

Matthew 7:21 - Not everyone that saith unto me, Lord, Lord, shall enter into the kingdom of heaven; but he that doeth the will of my Father which is in heaven.

James 1:22 - But be ye doers of the word, and not hearers only, deceiving your own selves.

Isaiah 1:19 - If ye be willing and obedient, ye shall eat the good of the land:

1 Samuel 15:22 - And Samuel said, Hath the LORD [as great] delight in burnt offerings and sacrifices, as in obeying the voice of the LORD? Behold, to obey [is] better than sacrifice, [and] to hearken than the fat of rams.

Ephesians 6:5-9 - Servants, be obedient to them that are [your] masters according to the flesh, with fear and trembling, in singleness of your heart, as unto Christ; 6 Not with eyeservice, as men pleasers; but as the servants of Christ, doing the will of God from the heart;7 With good will doing service, as to the Lord, and not to men:8 Knowing that whatsoever good thing any man doeth, the same shall he receive of the Lord, whether he be bond or free.9 And, ye masters, do the same things unto them, forbearing threatening:

knowing that your Master also is in heaven; neither is there respect of persons with him.

Romans 8:28 - And we know that all things work together for good to them that love God, to them who are the called according to [his] purpose.

James 2:24 - Ye see then how that by works a man is justified, and not by faith only.

John 14:21 - He that hath my commandments, and keepeth them, he it is that loveth me: and he that loveth me shall be loved of my Father, and I will love him, and will manifest myself to him.

Matthew 7:14 - Because strait [is] the gate, and narrow [is] the way, which leadeth unto life, and few there be that find it.

DECISION TIME

FOR THE LORD YOUR GOD IS
GRACIOUS AND MERCIFUL, AND WILL
NOT TURN AWAY HIS FACE FROM
YOU, IF YE RETURN UNTO HIM.
2CHRONICLES 30:9B

Will You Dedicate Your Life To Jesus Christ Today?

> That if thou shalt confess with thy mouth the LORD Jesus, and shalt believe in thine heart that God hath raised him from the dead, thou shalt be saved.
>
> **ROMANS 10:9**

If you have never **accepted Jesus Christ** as your personal Lord and Savior, you can make this important choice today. Also, if you have given your life to Jesus Christ but engaged in ways that are not pleasing to Him, you can take this time to **repent** and **rededicate** your life.

God desires that all should be saved (1Timothy 2:4). Know that there is no sin that can separate you from the love of God. You mean more to Him than your sins and faults, that is why He sent Jesus to die on the cross for the sins of humanity.

God desires for you to come to Him just the way that you are. He loves you and wants you to live a life of salvation, however the decision is yours.

If you want to accept Jesus Christ as your personal savior or wish to rededicate your life say this simple prayer today!

Father who art in heaven, I repent of all my sins, known and unknown and ask your forgiveness for the things I have done in disobedience. On this day(_____) and at this present time(_____), it is my desire to receive salvation. Today I accept Jesus Christ as my personal Lord and Savior and ask that you come into my life and cleanse me of every sinful behavior that would create a barrier between my relationship with you. Help me to walk in your grace, faith and mercy according to the redemption Jesus Christ has provided for me on the cross. May I become a better me in you, that I can prosper and live a life you desire for me, in Jesus' Name, Amen.

----

o Yes, Vincent! I have accepted Jesus Christ as my Lord and Savior today. Please send me my free gift.

Name: _____

Address: _____

City: _____ State: _____

Phone: _____

Email: _____

Mail form to:
Generation of Faith Foundation
P.O. Box 15462
Richmond Virginia 23227

ABOUT THE AUTHOR

Vincent K. Kpodo is the founder of Generation of Faith Foundation; a prayer and compassionate ministry committed to transforming lives and making the lifestyle of prayer an attractive one to many.

He was born into a Catholic home but later on in life started indulging in occultism in search of the true power of God. About two and a half years into occultism, he was struck down by a liver dysfunction which almost led to the point of his death. It was at that point on his bed of affliction he encountered Jesus Christ and received his call into ministry.

A major part of his assignment is to induct the 'act of prayer' in the lives of believers across the world, raise leaders and transform lives. Although the road has not always been smooth, his ministry has and continues to transform thousands of lives around the world; following signs, wonders, miracles and other notable testimonies.

His passion for serving humanity is not only evident in ministry but, has also been practically reflected in his **over ten years of honorable service in the United States Military** during a time of intensive war.

Vincent is currently married to Amanda and they are both blessed with their beautiful daughter Tehillah and many more to come.

Follow Vincent on :

Instagram:@ vincentkpodo

Facebook:@Vincent.K.Kpodo

Twitter:@vincentkpodo

Periscope:@vincentkpodo